Job-Shadowing

Daniel

Endorsements

In this superbly illustrated book Larry Peabody has gone a large step forward from his earlier volume on how everyday work is full-time ministry. Peabody has found in the biblical story of Daniel a mentor to illuminate and empower us to see our contemporary workplace situation, largely post-Christian or non-Christian, as an arena for faith development, for full-time ministry, and for kingdom witness. He views today's Daniels as people by and large doing good work and so fulfilling the creation mandate to develop the potential of creation. More than that, a biblical work-view enables us to see how both God and neighbor are being loved through our work, so fulfilling the great commandments. But finally through faith people in the workplace can reflect the image of God and be God's ambassadors in the most significant arena for kingdom mission in the twenty-first century—the workplace. I wish every Christian working in the world, and every pastor, would read this book and gain this transformed and transformative vision.

R. Paul Stevens

Professor Emeritus, Marketplace Theology, Regent College, Vancouver, BC

Author, *Doing God's Business* and *The Other Six Days*

Larry Peabody embodies what he has written. After working in a "secular" position for a couple of decades he moved into a "sacred" position and planted and pastored a thriving church. With keen insight, he dismantles the myth that a secular job cannot be a sacred ministry. He makes Daniel, whose service to God 2600 years ago through influential positions within a pagan culture, a powerful role model to all who work daily in positions outside the four walls of the church. Both provocative and empowering, this book offers an essential resource for market place ministries, one of the great movements that God has raised up in our day.

Leland V. Eliason

Executive Director and Provost Emeritus

Bethel Seminary of Bethel University

I am honored to endorse Larry Peabody's new book, *Job-Shadowing Daniel: Walking the Talk at Work.* It was Peabody's first book, *Secular Work is Full-Time Service*, which brought great clarity to my own work career. I still have my copy from the '70s, its yellowed pages replete with extensive underlining and marginal notes. Now, as with his first book, Peabody draws from the extraordinary life of Daniel, but here as workplace mentor. You will see its direct application to your daily work in Babylon. This succinct and practical guide will still speak to me decades from now. May it become your close companion as well!

John D. Beckett

Chairman, The Beckett Companies, Elyria, Ohio

Author: *Loving Monday* and *Mastering Monday*

Job-Shadowing Daniel

Walking the Talk at Work

Larry Peabody

Outskirts Press, Inc.
Denver, Colorado

Contents

FOREWORD

"Someday I'm going to quit my job and go into the ministry!"

Have you ever heard a statement like that? Maybe you have heard the testimony of a pastor or a missionary who actually did quit his or her job "to go into the ministry."

Those who make such career choices are often highlighted in church services as exemplary models. They are brought before the congregation, and commissioned for "the ministry." While it is important to pray for such people when the congregation gathers, the fact that civil servants, engineers, and real estate agents are not among the commissioned sends a regrettable message. The message is: "If you really want to serve the Lord, you'll be a pastor, a missionary or you'll do some kind of church-related work."

But as Larry Peabody explained so well in his first book, *Secular Work Is Full-time Service* (now titled, *Serving Christ in the Workplace*), all followers of Christ are called into full-time Christian service. Whether we are working in retail sales, farming or manufacturing, it is the Lord Christ whom we serve.

I am delighted that after thirty-five years, Larry has now carried the theme of his first book to an even greater height and depth in his second, *Job-Shadowing Daniel: Walking the Talk at Work*. This book was worth the wait!

Larry's skill as a gifted expositor of truth comes through the pages with shining clarity, and the book has a timely sense of urgency. It is a message "for such a time as this."

The life of Daniel stands out as a compelling example of what it means to serve the Lord through daily work in a culture that does not acknowledge the true living God. Today, our own culture is heading away from this acknowledgement with remarkable speed.

Babylon was far from Jerusalem, not only geographically, but socially and spiritually. It was a society built upon false gods, and it was full of the many challenges that come with a culture that normalizes idolatry. Yet, there was no better place for Daniel to be working. His example is especially relevant, for we live in a society where the continuous babble of people who have removed God from their thinking is heard all around us.

We need Larry's message. It is my hope that *Job-Shadowing Daniel* will be widely read, not only by individuals, but as a repeated study in churches and schools. The discussion questions at the end of each chapter make *Job-Shadowing Daniel* ideal for group use.

Larry Peabody is particularly qualified to write this book. For eleven years, he served the Lord as a government employee of the State of Washington, followed by seventeen years as a small business owner. In addition, Larry served for eight years as a bivocational pastor, and thirteen years as a full-time senior pastor.

I have travelled with Larry, shared meals with him and his lovely wife, Sharon, and taught with him side by side. He is a humble man of authentic integrity, and I commend him to you without reservation.

Dr. Christian Overman
Founding Director, Worldview Matters
Author, *Assumptions That Affect Our Lives, God's Pleasure at Work: Bridging the Sacred-Secular Divide*, and *The Difference One Life Can Make: Experiencing God's Pleasure at Work*
www.worldviewmatters.com

Introduction

WHY DANIEL? WHY NOW?

Daniel's well known face-off with the lions resulted from what he faced in his workplace. Although they'll never appear in a zoo, your workplace "lions" can be just as daunting as those in that ancient den.

There's the lion of *legalistic separation*. It roars that the work world is too polluted for Christian habitation. The lion of *religious tradition* tears the world and its work into "sacred" and "secular" pieces and urges you to think your work has little or no value in God's eyes. Always lurking in the background is the lion of *diminished identity*. It tries to neutralize you with the idea that you're just a layperson, not called for any real ministry. Other lions come in the form of *unbelieving co-workers,* some of whom will target any believer who dares to take a stand for Christ in the workplace. Behind these and any others is the *enemy lion* (or the *lyin' enemy*) on the prowl for someone to devour with his temptations and accusations.

Would Jesus actually position his followers among such beasts? He didn't speak of lions, as such. But he did compare our situation with that of lambs among wolves. He also told his disciples, "You are the light of the world." Then he sent them into that world.

Who could have guessed that countless non-Christians would pick up the tab for our going exactly where he sends us? And when an unbelieving employer hires a Christ-follower, another agent of Jesus goes into the world—the work world. With such great numbers of believers in the work force, why then does so much of the world remain unlit? Could it be that far too few Christian believers see themselves as Jesus' agents sent to live out their faith in their workplaces? And might the intimidating "lions," at least in part, account for that?

Daniel's Work Life Invites Job-Shadowing

Christians in the work world need models. They need to tag along after someone who faces the "lions" while trusting God. Daniel worked for a pagan government. Because the Bible provides many insights into his work life, it's possible for you to job-shadow him. Job-shadowing, according to one definition, "involves spending a period of time with a seasoned expert." This book will help you walk alongside Daniel, viewing his work life from a number of angles.

Hearing the title of that old song, "Dare to be a Daniel," you may wonder, *Who me? No way could I be Daniel. He wrote a book of the Bible. God gave him visions of the future. Jesus called him a "prophet." That's definitely not me!* Granted, you'll always be you. You'll never be Daniel. But take a moment to think through how much you and he have in common.

- Is your job what many today call "secular" work? Daniel worked on a government payroll, not for a religious organization. In current lingo, we'd label him a bureaucrat.
- Do unbelievers outnumber believers in your workplace? They did in Daniel's world, too. His job placed him as one of God's scattered people, far from the Holy City and its temple. Like Daniel, you probably work at a distance from the gathering of like-minded people.

- Do the values and behaviors typical of your work world seem confused, self-centered and opposed to God? Daniel worked in Babylon, a name related to "Babel," the city whose people had ambitions to build a heaven-reaching tower to make a name for themselves. God stopped them by confusing their languages, causing them to scatter far and wide. So "Babel" and "Babylon" speak of both rebellion and confusion.
- Does your faith sometimes make you a target for opposition on the job? So did Daniel's faith.
- Has God given you gifts and abilities that make you able to do your work? Daniel, too, was gifted by God to do the government work his bosses assigned to him.

Consider Daniel as Your Mentor.

The list of similarities could go on. But these five at least suggest that if you, as a Christian believer, are looking for a workplace mentor, you'd do well to consider Daniel. What he lived through qualifies him to serve as any working Christian's coach.

One major *difference* between you and Daniel also gives him an edge as a mentor-candidate. Daniel lived and worked some 600 years before the birth of Jesus. So he had not inherited the centuries of church tradition that have conditioned you and me to think of work as either "sacred" or "secular." Daniel did not see himself as "just a layperson." He did not dream of quitting his job to go into "full-time service."

Not many Christians, though, look to Daniel as a workplace mentor. I've recently spoken to Christians who told me it had been years since they had read the book of Daniel. And if the typical believer does think of Daniel, what comes to mind? To answer that, just ask the next ten Christians you meet, "What do you picture when someone mentions the Old Testament character, Daniel?" Most will probably say, "The lion's den." Follow up by asking, "How much time did Daniel spend among the lions?"

Some will recall he spent just one night there. Then ask, "How long did Daniel spend working for and among unbelievers?" I've found that few know his workplace experience probably spanned 70 years or more.

Without a doubt God performed a spectacular miracle by keeping those hungry lions from dining on Daniel. The story pulls us in with its danger and drama. We love stories of God supernaturally stepping in. But is Daniel's faithfulness over his decades-long career any less impressive?

Think of it. An enemy nation yanks a teenaged Jewish boy up by the roots, forcing him to leave his home, his parents and his Temple in Jerusalem. For the next month or more he travels as the captive of complete strangers to a land located more than 700 miles from home. His new boss orders his virtual brainwashing in the culture, practices and superstitions of this strange and godless environment. And then, despite all this, he serves the true God faithfully through one government regime after another—even being chosen to write a book in the Bible that still feeds God's people some 2,700 years later. In my mind, a career like that deserves a close look by contemporary believers serving in the workplaces of today's world.

Our 21st Century western culture continues to ratchet up its opposition to what Christians believe and stand for. Today, believers in offices, shops, schoolrooms, factories and fields are finding it increasingly difficult to sustain a godly presence in this Babylon-like confusion. But it's not just pressure from the world that makes working in these places tough for us. Much of the strain comes from our own lack of preparation for these assignments. Down deep, many of us aren't even sure we ought to be so "out there" in these "secular" places. Further, many of us find it hard to keep fixing our eyes on things above when our career demands that we focus on so many things here below.

Daniel Inspires Us to Become Workplace-Ready Disciples.

Our religious traditions have taught us to think of "ministry" in terms of church programs in special buildings and missionary activity on foreign soils. Those traditions have conditioned us to see credentialed "ministers" as the only ones suited for roles in "full-time Christian service." But our training has not readied us with a clear idea of what ministry looks like in the day-in-day-out flow of life in the work world where so many Christians spend so much time.

In his book, *God at Work*, David W. Miller reports that, "Generally speaking, neither the church nor the theological academy has had an intentional ministry or theological focus to help . . . those who work in the marketplace in their daily work." As a result, he says, "Many people in the marketplace turn to pop-culture solutions, self-help books, New Age spirituality, private piety, or Gnostic back-to-nature movements to find meaning and purpose in their lives. In the meantime, the church who has so much to offer sits on the sidelines with half-empty pews."

Before sending troops into harm's way, our military makes certain they are battle-ready. Christians in the world of work need to be workplace-ready. Daniel's experience as an administrator in an ungodly government can help you to prepare for facing those workplace lions.

Daniel Models Living as a Scattered People.

Daniel and the other transplanted Jews lived in the *diaspora*. This word, used in the Greek translation of Deut. 28:25, means a *scattering of seeds*. After conquering the Jewish homeland, the invaders flung its people far and wide. This scattering had long-lasting consequences. Hundreds of years later, when Jesus said he would go where people could not find him, the Jews asked, "Will he go where our people live scattered among the Greeks [literally, the *Diaspora*]?" (Jn. 7:35). When Daniel went to work each day, he did so as one of God's seeds scattered into soil that until then had produced only weeds. By job-shadowing Daniel in his workplace, scattered believers can learn how to turn "secular" jobs into ministry—and to do so over the long haul.

Today, when you get up and head for work, you—like Daniel— scatter as one of God's seeds. Jesus once told a parable about a farmer who flung seed into his field. The disciples missed the point. So Jesus explained, "The one who sowed the good seed is the Son of Man. The field is the world, and the good seed stands for the sons of the kingdom" (Matt. 13:37-38). The church is not only *ekklesia*—a gathered people. It is also *diaspora*—a scattered-seed people. We Christians have spent time, money and effort on buildings and methods to serve us when we *gather*. But we have done little to equip ourselves with the tools we need to live as kingdom-seeds when we *scatter*. As a Christian, you are there in your workplace because Jesus sowed you there as a seed. A seed carries life meant to develop into a fruit-producing plant where it lands. Daniel's example can help you learn how to live and work as a scattered seed.

Daniel Demonstrates Ministry in the Workplace.

In *God at Work*, Miller mentions a document that summarizes 50 years of social-witness statements by a major denomination. "In terms of substance," he says, "the policy papers are largely oriented to macro policy and structural questions, usually pertaining to issues of economic justice, sustainable development, offshore manufacturing, and third world debt forgiveness. However, they seldom speak to the level of individual vocation, accountability, and responsibility in the marketplace. Even the statements that attempt to move to the micro or personal level seldom apply to the average businessperson or worker in the pew."

Most of us do not work in jobs that require us to make high-level policy decisions with global implications. Daniel's ministry took shape in the context of such day-to-day, up-close issues as lifestyle, office politics and personal relationships. By focusing on his work life, this book aims to help you develop ministries that take place at that "micro," down-to-earth level.

Daniel Directs Our Eyes to Jesus.

But Daniel provides even more than examples, instruction and encouragement. Like Abraham and Isaiah, he foresaw the Coming One, the one who would be "like a son of man, coming with the clouds of heaven" (Dan. 7:13). The risen Jesus, while speaking with two followers on the road to Emmaus, started with Moses and all the Prophets as "he explained to them what was said in all the Scriptures concerning himself" (Luke 24:27). So as a part of Scripture, the book of Daniel reveals Christ.

In many ways, Daniel's life foreshadows Jesus. We'll touch on some of those ways in the chapters that follow. Countless Christians will run many miles of the faith marathon right in their workplaces. How will they be able to stay in the race without "hitting the wall"? Only, as the writer of Hebrews reminds us, by fixing their eyes on Jesus (Heb. 12:2). Daniel's life provides a lens through which you can see Jesus more clearly, even as you run the faith-race in your workplace.

This book visits some of the incidents from Daniel's life in the workplace more than once. Why? Because multiple insights emerge from the same experience. In the New Testament, both Hebrews and James refer to Abraham placing his son Isaac on the sacrificial altar—yet each writer extracts from that story a different truth. The gospel of John, Acts, I Corinthians and Hebrews all mention the experience of Israel in the desert, each drawing from it a fresh lesson. For anyone willing to take the time to mine it closely, each incident Daniel lived through in the workplace will usually pay off with multiple nugget-filled layers.

No, you'll never *be* Daniel. But will you dare to let him mentor you?

PART **I**

GETTING SETTLED IN BABYLON

Living as a Christ-follower in the world-system should put us in tension. Jesus sends us into the world, yet tells us we are not of it. We have homes on earth, yet we are not at home in this world. We're neighbors and co-workers, while at the same time aliens and strangers. Like violin strings, without this tension we can never sound the notes the world needs to hear.

Yet living in tension does not mean living tensely. Daniel and the Jewish exiles knew God had sent them into Babylon for 70 years. We Christians don't know how long our stay on this earth will last. But like those exiles, we need to settle down and live where God has sent us.

Sadly, many Christians in the workplaces of this world remain unsettled. Some live with divided minds, haunted by the suspicion they should quit their jobs and enter "full-time Christian service." The work-world itself can be unsettling. The wonders of its technology and the lure of its promise of wealth or status overcome many and leave them unproductive for God. These don't settle, they sink. Others—afraid of the world's power to corrupt—find it nerve-racking to interact with the world much at all. So, like the airline passenger terrified of flying, they never put their whole weight down in the workplace.

The four chapters in Part One address these settling-down concerns. Chapter One raises the question of calling. Does God call people into the world's workplaces or just into religious occupations? Chapter Two explores what kept Daniel from getting overly impressed—and swallowed up—by the dazzling sights and sounds of Babylon. Chapter Three shows how Daniel's certainty about his own identity made him able to resist attacks on it and to settle down even though surrounded by ungodly people. In Chapter Four, you'll follow Daniel as he practices separation, but does so in a non-legalistic way that preserves relationships with unbelievers.

Like Daniel, we expect our inheritance from outside the world's system. Meanwhile, we need to plant our feet in Babylon and live real lives while we're here.

CHAPTER ONE

CALLING: WORKING IN THE WORLD WHOLEHEARTEDLY

"Relatively few churches and pastors are reinforcing the legitimacy of a call into so-called 'secular work.' I have colleagues with tremendous business influence who are starving spiritually in their local churches. There's zero feeding; there's zero reinforcing of the call they have in the marketplace."
   John D. Beckett, Interview, "Christianity Today"

"Clericalism, or the belief that those in vocational ministry have a higher status or spiritual value, is a foundational assumption in many churches."
   Darrell Cosden, the Heavenly Good of Earthly Work

Framing the Issue: If you're a Christian in a "secular" job, have you sometimes wondered if you've missed God's best? Should you have gone overseas as a missionary? Or served as a church pastor? Did you fail to hear "the call"? This occupational inferiority complex infects believers around the world. It can keep you from doing your everyday work "wholeheartedly, as to the Lord." Although no heavenly voice called Daniel to government work in Babylon, he served God in that role—and did so full time.

Shall I continue in secular work or quit my job and enter full-time Christian service?

That question disturbs countless believers. An Internet blogger described his struggle in these words: *"I have been feeling like I should be doing something, but I just don't know what exactly that is. I don't know if I'm to leave my job and go into full-time missions."*

A friend of Darrell Cosden worked as a civil engineer. But, as Cosden reports in his book, *The Heavenly Good of Earthly Work,* his friend *"admitted that when he stands back and thinks about what he does every day, he often feels frustrated. He feels he is failing to make a contribution in really important spiritual matters."*

In a website article, Matthew Alexander wrote: *"When I was a student at the University of Kansas. . . I was under the false assumption that if I really wanted to please God and if I really wanted to do something of significance, then I needed to go into 'full-time ministry.' However, I didn't believe I was equipped for being a pastor or missionary, nor did I want to be. I shared this spiritual tension with friends from a campus ministry I attended and learned several of them also wrestled with the same tension."*

A Focus on the Family article by Dr. Walt Larimore tells of Tom, a young Christian who started a business in which employees and customers were coming to faith in Christ. Tom's pastor, recognizing spiritual fruitfulness, asked, *"Tom, have you ever considered really giving your life to God—working full time for the Lord?"* Tom said he thought he was already doing so. *"Tom,"* the pastor continued, *"there's no doubt that God has used you in amazing ways; but the work you're in is secular. I think God is calling you to consider becoming involved in something higher."*

The horns of this same dilemma skewered me early on. Raised in a strongly evangelical home and church, I soon learned the lingo: *full-time service, real live missionary, reverend* and so on. When I was about 12, our pastor's wife told me—at their farewell event—that she expected to hear great things from me in years to come. Even as a pre-teen, I knew how to translate those "great things" code words. She meant she expected me to become a pastor or missionary. But in college, I began examining my motives. Like Jeremiah's secretary, Baruch, I was seeking those "great things" for myself. It dawned on me that I had seen those religious roles as stairways to significance and recognition within the Christian community—and my own motives appalled me.

One day I sat down and wrote out my argument with God over this issue. Wanting my life to matter, I urgently made my case for "full-time Christian service." But God kept urging me to enter the world of "secular" work. No, I wrote. I'd get swallowed up. Get lost in the 9-5 shuffle. Disappear in the crowd, never to be noticed again. But God was assuring me he could still use me there if I had the patience to wait and see.

A few years later, after moving to a new town, I began working for a government agency, and we joined a local church. One Sunday morning, the pastor urged us all to return that evening to hear a speaker. "He has a wonderful testimony," the pastor said, "even though he's just a layman." Just. Merely. Here it was again—the Christian caste system that assigns most Christians to the minor leagues and a tiny few to the majors. On Mother's Day, the same pastor called to the platform those mothers who had children in the pastorate or on the mission field. Each received applause and a corsage. I sat there painfully aware of other mothers in the room who had reared wonderful Christians now serving as teachers, state employees and truck drivers. Where, I wondered, were their orchids?

What unplugs Sunday from Monday?

What's behind the disconnect between sacred and secular, between church and work? On one hand, the world works at pulling them apart. For example, in the movie, *Expelled*, P. Z.

Myers, a biology professor, tries to drive a wedge between Sunday and Monday. In his words: *"We're not going to take away their churches. But what we have to do is get into a place where religion is treated at the level it should be treated, that is, something fun that people get together and do on the weekend and really doesn't affect their life as much as it has . . . ."* The unbelieving world wants to quarantine Christian influence inside the "sacred" weekend gatherings to keep it from infecting the "secular" world where people live and work. No big surprise.

On the other hand—and more disturbing—our own church traditions widen the gulf by exalting the sacred above the secular. If you've attended evangelical churches for any length of time, you've probably heard testimonies along the lines of this actual example from a church leader: *"I recall that when God called me into full-time service, I struggled to give up my comfortable career as I was really not ready then. I remembered trying to compromise with the Lord by telling Him that I would continue to love and serve Him, but not give up my job and move into full-time ministry. In other words, I was telling the Lord that I preferred my way rather than His purpose in my life."*

Sort out the either-or contrasts assumed in this testimony. It's either "full-time service" for God or "my comfortable career." It's either "give up my job" or "compromise." It's either "ministry" or "my job." It's either full-time service as God's "purpose for my life" or "my way." The testimony begins with the church leader remembering "when God called me into full-time service." This statement implies two things. First, *although a Christian before God called me, I was not in full-time service.* And second, *it was God's call that thrust me into full-time service.* Who can miss the point that those in *full-time service* are the ones God has *called*?

Many Christian leaders communicate the same message. For example: *"If we are committed to the mission God calls us to it will cost us in time, in prayer, and in finance. But maybe there is another area where God wants to challenge you tonight. Life. Maybe he wants your life. And by that I mean maybe he wants you to quit secular work—to give up being 'normal' and commit your life to the mission—to become a missionary . . . ."* Implication: Giving God your life means quitting your job to become a missionary.

Another example: *"In 1989 I answered God's call to ministry and left secular work."* In citing these examples, I am not denying that God directs some people to pastoral and missionary roles. He has and does. My point is that our words create the false impression that those are the *only* believers with a call of God on their lives and work. R. Paul Stevens observes, ". . . almost the only people who speak of being 'called of God' are 'full-time' missionaries and pastors" (*The Other Six Days*). As a result, Stevens says, "Few business people . . . think of themselves as full-time ministers in the marketplace."

Those who offer testimonies like those quoted above may not realize their words actually hinder typical Christians from thinking of themselves as full-time ministers where they work. Imagine the thoughts of "Joe," a government auditor, after listening to the Christian who finally gave in by entering "full-time service." Suddenly Joe begins to see his own job as spiritually second-rate. So far as he knows, God has never called him to leave his work with the state. Yet as this testimony echoes in his ears, his everyday work now seems a daily surrender to selfishness—just a cushy career. By sticking with his auditing job, is he choosing his own way over God's purpose for his life?

Joe hears the same theme not just once, but again and again from dedicated believers. So he begins to suspect his lack of a *call* makes him one of the *uncalled*. Such testimonies always associate calling with ministry. Connecting the dots, he concludes God has not called him to ministry. Then, too, the experiences of certain Bible characters seem to reinforce the idea that any "call" from God always comes with awesome special effects. Take Isaiah. His assignment came with a vision of the Lord on a high and exalted throne. Or Paul. A light struck him to the ground and left him blind for three days. Nothing of that sort has ever happened to Joe, the auditor. Further evidence in Joe's mind that God has never called him to full-time ministry.

Imagine what Joe would have taken away had he attended a memorial service for a Bible Institute professor in which one of his former students said: *"We are ever indebted to them* [the professor and his wife] *for being used of God to lead us out of secular work into full-time ministry."* Apparently "secular work" is something Joe should be thankful to be led out of!

How Daniel Got His Job.

But wait! Some of God's most dedicated servants in the Bible never received any spectacular call. Daniel was neither a missionary nor a pastor. He worked for the government of Babylon. In this and the following chapters, we're going to watch Daniel in his workplace. Why? Because he knew how to connect his faith with his everyday work. His example can show you how to do that too. In this chapter we'll look at how Daniel got into his job as a Babylonian bureaucrat. Did God call him to such work? If so, what did his "call" look like? Let's look for answers in Dan. 1:1-7.

> *In the third year of the reign of Jehoiakim king of Judah, Nebuchadnezzar king of Babylon came to Jerusalem and besieged it. And the Lord delivered Jehoiakim king of Judah into his hand, along with some of the articles from the temple of God. These he carried off to the temple of his god in Babylonia and put in the treasure house of his god. Then the king ordered Ashpenaz, chief of his court officials, to bring in some of the Israelites from the royal family and the nobility—young men without any physical defect, handsome, showing aptitude for every kind of learning, well informed, quick to understand, and qualified to serve in the king's palace. He was to teach them the language*

and literature of the Babylonians. The king assigned them a daily amount of food and wine from the king's table. They were to be trained for three years, and after that they were to enter the king's service. Among these were some from Judah: Daniel, Hananiah, Mishael and Azariah. The chief official gave them new names: to Daniel, the name Belteshazzar; to Hananiah, Shadrach; to Mishael, Meshach; and to Azariah, Abednego.

These verses tell us exactly when Daniel began working for the government of Babylon: ". . . in the third year of Jehoiakim king of Judah." In our terms, that was 605 years before Jesus' birth. From v. 4 we know Daniel began his career early, as one among a number of "young men." He was probably a teenager.

Back in Judah, before coming to Babylon, Daniel may have known Jeremiah, the outspoken prophet who had infuriated Jewish leaders for at least 20 years. Through Jeremiah, God had foretold exactly what would happen if the nation continued her unfaithfulness: "I will hand you over to those who seek your life, those you fear — to Nebuchadnezzar king of Babylon and to the Babylonians. I will hurl you and the mother who gave you birth into another country, where neither of you was born, and there you both will die. You will never come back to the land you long to return to" (Jer. 22:25-27).

And now, in this year of 605 B.C., politically incorrect prophecies such as this one were proving true. Verse 1 sums it up: "Nebuchadnezzar king of Babylon came to Jerusalem and besieged it." Verses 3 and following describe the results of this assault. First, the Jewish king, Jehoiakim, became Nebuchadnezzar's underling. Second, Nebuchadnezzar confiscated some of the sacred temple articles, hauled them off to Babylon and displayed them as trophies in the temple of his false god. And third, he carted off the cream of the crop of Jewish young men and deported them to Babylon. There these young apprentices would be trained to work in Nebuchadnezzar's government. Among those young men was Daniel. So far as we know, Daniel never returned to his homeland. He spent his entire career as a government worker in Babylon.

Did God Call Daniel to Work in Babylon?

As we've seen, Daniel may well have known Jeremiah. Maybe he had even heard Jeremiah testify about his call. What if Daniel had compared his own situation with Jeremiah's? To Jeremiah, God had said, "Before I formed you in the womb I knew you, before you were born I set you apart; I appointed you as a prophet to the nations" (Jer. 1:5). Now that's drama, to have God single you out and tell you his purpose for your life. By contrast, Daniel's place seems to have come about as a mere accident of war. It looks as if Daniel has not been placed but *displaced*. Suppose Daniel had said to himself: "Jeremiah heard God's voice call him; I heard no voice. Jeremiah's call made him a prophet; my circumstances made me into a bureaucrat. I guess God hasn't called me into ministry."

God's General Call—Purpose. If Daniel had concluded he was one of the uncalled and so not in ministry, would he have been right? Perhaps we need to think again about what it means to be called of God. When God calls, he summons. He urgently invites. If you're a Christian believer, you became one because you said yes to God's call to turn from your sin and self-trust and to place your faith in his Son, Jesus. As I Pet. 2:9 puts it, "God . . . called you out of darkness into his wonderful light." That's God's general call. All Christians share this call. Although the Bible does not include the term "full-time service," it leaves no doubt that God's general call to all Christians is a call to serve him full time. For example, Paul, writing to everyone in the church at Corinth, instructed them to "Always give yourselves fully to the work of the Lord" (I Cor. 15:58). To what extent were they to devote themselves to the Lord's work? Always. Fully. That sounds very much like full-time service.

Hold on, Paul! Many of these Corinthian Christians were slaves. How could you have expected *them* to give themselves *always* and *fully* to the work of the Lord? If those slaves had held the view many Christians hold today, this word through Paul would have caused some heartburn. Imagine a household slave assigned to manage his master's property saying to himself: "I wish I could do as Paul has written and give myself always and fully to the work of the Lord. But I'm stuck here in these household chores, so I guess all I can do is encourage other believers when we get together." Fortunately, those slaves had not inherited the centuries of church traditions that now condition believers to think in such ways. Paul—and they—understood that their slave work was all a part of their doing the "work of the Lord." God had summoned them to serve him in every part of their lives, all a part of his general call, all a part of his *purpose* that they bear fruit "in every good work" (Col. 1:10).

God's Specific Call—Placement. But God also issues a specific call. This call relates to his individual *placement* for each of his children. For example, Paul was "called to be an apostle" (Rom. 1:1; I Cor. 1:1). In calling him to be an apostle (one sent out with a message), God assigned Paul to a certain kind of work. This call even revealed he would work with a certain group of people— Gentiles (Acts 22:21). But his specific call to apostleship did not launch him into full-time service. That was part of his general call—one received by all believers. Paul continued to serve Christ full time even while engaged in the "secular" business of making tents. So when that church leader said, "God called me into full time service," he was confusing his general call with a specific call. God had already summoned him into full-time service with his general call to become a believer.

How do the general and specific calls fit together? Think of it this way. Suppose a couple purchases a fast-food franchise. To get their new business up and running, they put ten employees on the payroll. This hiring is their *general call*. As they get to know the employees, they assign two to run the grill, one to keep the place clean, three to take orders from customers and so on. Divvying up the work is the *specific call*. The owners purpose that each employee, everyone who received the general call, will work productively full time during his or her shift. In making the specific calls, they simply place each one in that part of the work he or she will specialize in. The employers do not make a distinction by saying that they called only some of the employees to work full-time during their hours on payroll. That would imply the others could spend only part of their shifts doing restaurant business and the rest of their time doing their own things.

What about Daniel's specific call? The Bible says nothing about him seeing any vision or hearing any voice from heaven. Instead, Daniel ended up in Babylon because, as we read in v. 2, "the Lord delivered Jehoiakim king of Judah into his [Nebuchadnezzar's] hand." Daniel's specific call, his placement, came as God summoned him through circumstances —painful circumstances. By means of those events, God placed Daniel in the work and in the workplace where he wanted him. For Daniel, that meant a job as a bureaucrat in Babylon.

Daniel's assignment runs parallel to that of another nearly 700 years later. Daniel sprang from the royal family (literally from "the king's seed," Dan. 1:3); Jesus was the royal Son of the Sovereign God. Daniel left behind the Holy City, the earthly temple with its Most Holy Place; Jesus came from the heavenly City with its eternal sanctuary and God's immediate presence. As God had sent Daniel into Babylon (land of darkness and confusion), he sent his Son Jesus into the devil's domain of this world. Through Daniel, God penetrated the darkened Babylonian government with light. Through Jesus, God infiltrated the whole world with light that continues to shine through his followers even today. As Jesus himself put it to his disciples, "You are the light of the world" (Matt. 5:14). And God's strategy, seen in Daniel and in Jesus, remains the same. Jesus summarized that strategy in prayer to his Father: "As you sent me into the world, I have sent them into the world" (Jn. 17:18). The "world" certainly includes the present-day world of work.

What About Your Work?

Is your so-called "secular" work second-best? You've had no dramatic call to work as a foreign missionary or church pastor. So does that exclude you from real ministry? Or does it limit you to "part-time ministry" crammed into evenings and weekends? Should you quit wasting your best hours and enter "full-time service"? Daniel's life and work can lead to several insights about your own situation today.

Trust God to place you where he wants you—even through your circumstances. God is sovereign. He has supreme power. He answers to no one. He can call you in any way he pleases, through words or through events as they unfold. In his sovereignty, God intervenes in the events of life on earth—just as he did in handing King Jehoiakim over to Nebuchadnezzar and, as a result, placing Daniel in a government career in Babylon.

God's sovereignty has everything to do with your specific call and with your everyday work. Like Joe the auditor, you may have felt uncalled. You've honestly never sensed God calling you to be a pastor, a foreign missionary or a traveling evangelist. So you may have concluded that you are not called to full-time ministry. But such a conclusion no longer makes sense when you realize that God, who is sovereign, works not only through dramatic encounters but also through your ordinary life circumstances.

Think of the work you do day after day. How did you come into that role and those responsibilities? Maybe it was the circumstance of *opportunity*—the job just opened up. Maybe it was the circumstance of *economic necessity*—the bills had to be paid and the kids needed food and clothing. The circumstance of *where you live* may have played a part in the daily work you now do. Or the circumstance of your *God-given gifts and abilities.*

Daniel 1:4 shows how the sovereign God used Daniel's gifts and abilities in calling him to Babylon. Daniel was one of those "young men who were healthy and handsome, intelligent and well-educated, good prospects for leadership positions in the government, perfect specimens" (*The Message*). Those were the very qualities Ashpenaz, Nebuchadnezzar's "head-hunter," looked for in candidates for relocation to Babylon and its bureaucracy. Why, then, should it surprise you if the sovereign God has used your unique qualities in positioning you where you work?

During my college years, I discovered God had given me a flair for writing. I actually enjoyed this activity so many had learned to hate during high school English classes! So I cultivated my writing skills, and even spent a couple of years as a free-lance writer. As it turned out, a state agency was looking for someone with writing ability—and through that circumstance God led me into work for the government as a public information officer for the next 11 years. These years turned out to be just as much a part of God's plan as those I spent in the role of a pastor on a church staff.

God's sovereignty shines through in Rom. 8:28: "And we know that in all things God works for the good of those who love him, who have been called according to his purpose." If you love the God who has called you to himself in Jesus, then count on this: God works for your good *in all things*. Even—as Daniel found—in the things that hurt. Believe that your work has come to you because God has been at work in the *all things* of your circumstances. No matter how it may have come, your specific calling is just as precious, just as important, as any other. Why? Because it has come to you from the God who intervenes in all circumstances for the good of those who love him.

Transform your job into full-time service. Just because a "secular" job slot is filled by a Christian does not automatically make it full-time service. If your job is to become part of your full-time service for God and others, you will have to convert it into that.

At one stage in Daniel's career, King Darius appointed three top-level administrators to oversee 120 officials. Daniel filled one of these administrator positions. Pagans almost certainly filled the other two. Although their job descriptions matched Daniel's, and although they were serving God unknowingly, their work could hardly have been called "full-time service" for the true God. Only Daniel's job was done as part of his God-centered full-time service. It takes a full-time servant of God to turn a job into full-time service for God. Following Daniel's stay in the lion's den, King Darius—who had spent a sleepless night worrying about Daniel's safety—came to the den and spoke to Daniel of "your God, whom you serve *continually*" (6:20, emphasis added). So even this pagan king could see that Daniel served God full time while doing his government work.

But "full-time service" in a regular job does not mean doing religious things on company time. Conditioned by years in our religious traditions, we might mistakenly try to make workplace ministry look and sound like church programs. In February 2004, *USA Today* carried the story of an American Airlines pilot, a Christian, who attempted to do what he saw as "ministry" while on a flight from Los Angeles to New York. He came on the intercom and said, "We've just leveled off at our cruising altitude, folks. According to our computer, we're anticipating an on-time arrival in New York. And now, I'd like all Christians to raise their hands." He went on to tell of a short-term mission he'd taken part in and then encouraged passengers to discuss religion. Understandably, passengers complained. After an internal investigation, the airline suspended the pious pilot.

In later chapters, we'll see more specifically how Daniel turned his job into full-time service in ways that did not get him suspended.

Recognize the value of your unique place in the work world. Chad Brewer gets it. He writes, "For many years, like most ministers, my dream was to become full time in ministry. The idea actually consumed me. I believed that in order to gain the respect that a minister deserved, you had to be full time. However, after much study, my views have somewhat changed. I have learned that we are 'all' to be ministers of the gospel, regardless of position or title, and I can be no more effective to the kingdom of God than when I am at work. Just think about it, how many people do we come in contact with on a day-to-day basis? . . . I have decided that (unless God says otherwise) I will continue to work in my marketplace and try to represent Christ to the very best of my ability in order to advance the kingdom of God."

Our religious traditions too easily lead us to think of "secular" work as second-rate or a waste of time. But Daniel's long career as a Babylonian bureaucrat should cure us of that kind of distorted vision. Because Daniel served God "continually" in his government job, he accomplished things Jeremiah could never have done in his speaking and writing ministry back in the Holy Land.

Through Daniel and his work God's light penetrated the pagan darkness of the Babylonian bureaucracy—something out of Jeremiah's reach. Because of Daniel, even Nebuchadnezzar, ruler of the world-empire, praised the true God. After Daniel told him his dream and its interpretation, this pagan ruler acknowledged: "Surely your God is the God of gods and the Lord of kings" (Dan. 2:47). And a later king, Darius, after seeing God deliver Daniel from hungry lions, said: "I issue a decree that in every part of my kingdom people must fear and reverence the God of Daniel. For he is the living God and he endures forever; his kingdom will not be destroyed, his dominion will never end. He rescues and he saves; he performs signs and wonders in the heavens and on the earth. He has rescued Daniel from the power of the lions" (Dan. 6:26-27).

Jesus would later call this bureaucrat, Daniel, a "prophet" (Matt. 24:15), the same word God had used to describe Jeremiah. Daniel had just as much of a specific call or vocation from God as Jeremiah. Yes, his call came less dramatically. But the same God who spoke the words that placed Jeremiah arranged the circumstances that placed Daniel in a government job in Babylon. Do we love the drama or do we love the God who positions us in whatever way he may choose?

In your so-called "secular" work, you can do what no pastor or missionary could ever do. "You," Jesus said to his followers, "are the light of the world." And so you, as you follow him, are one of his lights sent to illuminate a unique dark corner of the work world. Such work is clearly vital to God's strategy. It is not second-best. So you can do it—as Paul told Christians in the first-century workplace—"heartily, as Christ's servants" (Eph. 6:7, *The Message*).

The work world, though, can dazzle and deceive you. It seems to promise so much. As we'll see in the next chapter, young Daniel encountered in Babylon a world with far more outward pizzazz than the one he had known back home. But he stood firm in his faith because his God-given vision let him see beyond the glamour of his new world.

Putting It to Work

- Give a specific example or two of how you have experienced the Sunday-Monday gap.
- Before you read this chapter, how had you thought of your so-called "secular" work in terms of its value to the kingdom of God?
- In your own words, describe how this chapter explains the difference between God's general call and his specific call. Do you agree or disagree? Tell why.
- How did you come to have your present job? Do you see the hand of God at work in that process? Explain.
- What unique opportunities does your job offer for advancing God's agenda on earth?

CHAPTER TWO

VISION: SEEING THE BIG PICTURE

"Kingdom ministry has been almost totally eclipsed by church ministry."
    R. Paul Stevens, The Other Six Days:
    Vocation, Work and Ministry in Biblical Perspective

"The hope of the new kingdom is not that we will be released from work but rather that our work will be in perfect partnership with God in the kingdom that is yet to come."
    Gordon T. Smith, Courage and Calling

Framing the Issue: The world has many ways of capturing your attention and affection. Even Demas, one of Paul's own co-workers, "loved this world." The work world parades many lures and puts them within easy reach. Its bait includes power, money and knowledge. Unlike Demas, Daniel stood his ground against the pull of the world. Because he saw the eternal kingdom—he stayed true to its King decade after decade.

In the film, *Hoosiers,* actor Gene Hackman coaches the high school basketball team of Hickory, Indiana. The rural, small-town team makes it to the Indiana state finals. Most of these boys have never seen a building taller than two stories. As they walk from their bus into the massive arena, their mouths hang open as they take in its sheer size. Seeing their intimidated faces, Hackman pulls a tape measure from his pocket. He asks one boy to extend the tape from the free-throw line to just under the backboard. Fifteen feet. Then a second boy, on the shoulders of another, measures the distance between the floor and the hoop. Ten feet. I think you'll find, Hackman says, it's the same as our gym back in Hickory.

When Nebuchadnezzar transplanted him from Judah to Babylon, Daniel may well have felt much like those high school boys. But even a tape measure would not have helped. Jerusalem, the capital city of his homeland, may have had 25,000 people. By some estimates, the population of Babylon, capital city of the vast Babylonian empire, hit a half-million. This small-town boy, brought up to believe the true God, was now surrounded by powerful, rich and worldly-wise people. Daniel would spend his whole long career in this environment. Yet decades later, Daniel the senior citizen still trusted the true God as unflinchingly as he had in his youth. In spite of all the tempting detours in his workplace, Daniel finished well. What was his secret? Could knowing his secret make a difference in your life? Might Daniel's example help you stay spiritually strong even among the pressures where you work?

Babylon the Bedazzling.

Let's pull in for a closer look at Daniel's pagan workplace. Babylon was a world superpower. Encarta defines a superpower as, "an extremely powerful nation with greater political, economic, or military power than most other nations." That describes Babylon to a T. It sprawled from Egypt and the Mediterranean Sea north to the

Black Sea, east to the Caspian Sea and south to the Persian Gulf. With Nebuchadnezzar's triumph in Jerusalem, Daniel had seen up close the fearsome forces of Babylon in action. The Jewish state had caved under its crushing might. Once in Babylon, Daniel rose rapidly to the top ranks of government, so he soon had his hands on its levers of power.

Babylonian wealth must have seemed endless. As part of Nebuchadnezzar's government, Daniel watched the king transform the city into an architectural showplace. The Ishtar Gate, named after a goddess, may have stood 47 feet high and 100 feet wide. The bottom story of the Ziggurat (stepped like a wedding cake) measured 300 feet square. A temple capped its top story at 300 feet above the ground—making the temple of the true God back in Jerusalem look like a dollhouse. The Hanging Gardens of Babylon were considered one of the Seven Wonders of the World. According to Herodotus, a Greek historian of about 450 B.C., "Babylon surpasses in splendor any city in the known world." All these spectacular structures impressed even King Nebuchadnezzar. As he gazed on the city from his palace roof, he said, "Is not this the great Babylon I have built as the royal residence, by my mighty power and for the glory of my majesty?" (Dan. 4:30). Wealth made all this possible. As a top-level administrator, Daniel moved in these prosperous circles.

Babylonian knowledge ventured into areas well beyond the limits of Daniel's Jewish education. The book of Daniel refers repeatedly to the "wise men" of Babylon. That culture emphasized learning. In the ancient world, Babylon led the nations in astronomy. So, naturally, the Egyptians relied on Babylonian insight when they aligned their pyramids with the stars. But the learning also included astrology, the attempt to know how the stars influence human lives. And it covered magic, the art of prying open the invisible world to tap and use its secrets. According to Matthew Henry's Commentary, Daniel's Babylonian curricula included instruction "in the language and laws of the country, in history, philosophy, and mathematics, in the arts of husbandry, war, and navigation." This vast knowledge would equip Daniel to work as a government administrator. His new supervisors immediately immersed this small-town boy in the bragging point of their culture—"the language and literature of the Babylonians" (Dan. 1:4).

So Daniel left his sheltered Jewish culture and plunged into a world of power, money and learning. An old song, popular after World War I, asked: "How you gonna keep 'em down on the farm, after they've seen Paree [Paris]?" Knowing the sights that confronted Daniel in his new home, we might paraphrase the question: "How you gonna keep him firm in his faith, after he's seen Babylon?" Some today worry about the contemporary "Babylon" of the secular workplace. They warn Christians to steer clear of it. If seeing its tempting options might threaten their faith, shield them from the sight. Keep them faithful by keeping them out of the work world. Such a strategy, of course, flies in the face of Jesus who sends us into all the world. Daniel went right into the heart of the dark world. But instead of being overcome by darkness, Daniel shattered the darkness with God's light. What sustained him?

Kingdom-of-God Vision.

In large measure, *vision*. The Bible record leaves no doubt that this small-town boy lived with the vision of a kingdom that by comparison left the kingdom of Babylon looking like yesterday's leftovers. By faith, Daniel saw the kingdom of God, a kingdom that eclipsed even the most powerful, rich and sophisticated empire on earth. So he could look at Nebuchadnezzar's gigantic and expensive buildings—perhaps even help in arranging their construction—without oohing and ahhing. Daniel had Jesus' kind of vision. As they were leaving the temple in Jerusalem, one of Jesus' awestruck disciples said, "Look, Teacher! What massive stones! What magnificent buildings!" Ooh! Ahh! That's kingdom-of-this-world vision. Jesus answered: "Do you see all these great buildings? . . . Not one stone here will be left on another; every one will be thrown down" (Mk. 13:1-2). That's kingdom-of-God vision.

Daniel's kingdom vision foreshadows Jesus. In the four gospel accounts, Jesus speaks of the "Kingdom of God" or the "Kingdom of Heaven" more than 100 times. He mentions "church" twice. Jesus said the kingdom of God was to be seen, entered, sought and prayed for. He told parables to describe its unseen reality. He called the announcement of its nearness "good news." He said it was both near and coming. He told his followers to proclaim it. He said the end would come after the good news of the kingdom had been preached to the whole world. The kingdom, he said, was not of this world but from another place. He said people can be excluded from the kingdom—and that it's best to rid ourselves of anything that blocks us from it. He said his Father was giving the kingdom to his followers.

If Jesus thinks God's kingdom is this important, we'd best make sure we get what he means. In the United States, we live in a representative democracy (or a democratic republic), not in a kingdom. So it's easy for us to read "kingdom" and miss what Jesus meant. What is a kingdom? George Eldon Ladd, in *The Gospel of the Kingdom*, says both the Old and New Testament words for kingdom primarily mean "the authority to rule, the sovereignty of a king." Many of us may think of a kingdom in terms of physical territory or the population subject to a ruler. But Ladd points out that in Jesus' story in Lk. 19:12, a high-ranking man went into a distant country "to receive for himself a kingdom." He left the territory and the people over whom he would rule to receive the *kingdom*—the authority to rule over both. So the word "kingdom" refers in only a secondary sense to a geographic area or to the people of that area.

As Creator and Sustainer of the earth and all its creatures, God rightfully has the authority to rule as its sovereign. The Psalmist recognized this authority and called him, "the Lord Most High, the great King over all the earth" (Ps. 47:2)! God is the rightful Ruler of every square inch of earth's territory and every individual within the earth's population. But God chose not to rule his kingdom all alone, but to delegate some of his authority to deputy rulers. So just after creating them, God delegated authority to human beings to rule his earth under him. In God's words, "Let us make man in our image, in our likeness, and let them rule over . . . all the earth" (Gen. 1:26).

Selfishly ambitious Satan, however, saw his opportunity in these human beings God had deputized. In his encounter with Eve, he deceived them, diverted their allegiance from God to himself and in this way seized false authority. Humanity's misplaced loyalty allowed Satan to rule God's earth-rulers. On the basis of this power-grab, Satan set up his own rebel realm—what Paul refers to as the "kingdom of darkness" (Col. 1:13, NLT). Rev. 11:15 calls it the "kingdom of the world." The Bible often shortens this to simply "the world." That's why John wrote that "the whole world is under the control of the evil one" (I Jn. 5:19). God remains sovereign over his creation, but Satan rules the dark world-system of sin and death.

One of Jesus' parables—found in Mathew 21, Mark 12 and Luke 20—illustrates both God's sovereignty and Satan's takeover. A landowner planted a vineyard. While away on a trip, he put some tenant-farmers in charge of his property. At grape-harvest time, he sent some employees to collect what was due him. But the tenants repeatedly attacked and even murdered the landowner's bill-collectors. Thinking they would respect his son, the landowner sent him. But the tenants killed the son. Although a corrupt system temporarily ruled within the borders of that vineyard, the farm still belonged to the landowner. So he returned, executed the murderers and put others in charge of his property. Satan has set up his temporary world-system inside the creation that still belongs to the

God who is sovereign over it all. Satan's authority, unlike God's, is neither legitimate nor eternal. But to the extent that he can keep people dancing to his tune instead of getting into step with what God wants, he maintains control over his world-kingdom. Today, when anyone receives Jesus as God's rightful King and so enters into God's Kingdom, he or she is set free from the controller of the world-system.

Although living in the world-kingdom of Babylon, Daniel had 20/20 kingdom-of-God vision. How did he get such spiritual seeing ability? Trained from boyhood in the Jewish Scriptures, he had known of God's eternal kingdom before he ever set foot in Babylon. Moses, nearly a thousand years before Daniel, spoke of "the throne of the Lord" (Ex. 17:16). Four hundred years before Daniel's time, David, anticipating the coming Messiah, had written: "Your throne, O God, will last forever and ever" (Ps. 45:6). And Jeremiah, Daniel's contemporary, had written: "You, O LORD, reign forever; your throne endures from generation to generation" (Lam. 5:19). Daniel knew God's throne represented his sovereign authority to rule his creation.

Daniel's Babylon experiences confirmed and expanded his kingdom-of-God vision. In Daniel 2, Nebuchadnezzar, troubled by a dream, demands that his experts tell him both the dream and its meaning. After praying to the "God in heaven," Daniel does both. His interpretation describes four kingdoms. The first and most powerful is Babylon. The second, third and fourth kingdoms get progressively weaker. Then, says Daniel, "the God of heaven will set up a kingdom that will never be destroyed, nor will it be left to another people. It will crush all those kingdoms and bring them to an end, but it will itself endure forever" (Dan. 2:44).

In chapter 7, Daniel himself has a dream. Like Nebuchadnezzar's dream, its symbols speak of four world empires. Then after those kingdoms a fifth arises, and Daniel sees "one like a son of man, coming with the clouds of heaven" (7:13). Who is this "son of man"? Jesus answers this question for us: ". . . in the future you will see the Son of Man [Jesus himself] sitting at the right hand of the Mighty One and coming on the clouds of heaven" (Matt. 26:64). This fifth kingdom, Daniel heard, "will be handed over to the saints, the people of the Most High" (7:27).

Daniel's kingdom-of-God vision turns our paraphrase of the post-World-War-II song on its head. Now the question is: "How you gonna keep him down in Babylon, after he's seen the kingdom of God?" To Daniel, the power, the wealth and the learning of Babylon faded in light of the kingdom God had promised for the future. From the dreams of Nebuchadnezzar and Daniel, we can see that Daniel's kingdom-of-God vision includes at least five promises about the future. God's kingdom will:

- Be set up by God himself.
- Crush and end all man-made kingdoms.
- Last forever.
- Be ruled by "one like a son of man."
- Be given to his people.

Daniel, like Jesus, announced the coming kingdom of God. Both gave that kingdom top priority, just as we are to seek it first as we work in today's world. Daniel trusted God to carry through on these kingdom promises. This faith made him able to work in Babylon without letting it lure him into ruin. And this faith so illuminated his own soul that he could radiate God's light into the darkened lives of his co-workers.

Have those kingdom promises become obsolete? Were they valid only in Old Testament times? No way. Jesus and the New Testament clarify and amplify them. So much so that by counting on God to keep these same promises, you too can work in a "secular" job, stay faithful to Jesus and shine his light into that particular pocket of darkness. Let's look at the five promises and why you need to count on them.

God Himself Will Set up His Kingdom. Some 600 years

after Nebuchadnezzar heard Daniel's kingdom-of-God prophecy, Jesus announced the good news (literally "the gospel") that: "The kingdom of God is near." How? In the person of Jesus himself—God's anointed King. God's kingdom has invaded the devil's domain. God's kingdom is not yet visible to the physical eye. That outward phase of his kingdom is still to come. And come it will. But to those who receive and believe in Jesus, it is possible to "see" and to "enter" the kingdom of God now. You and I can now enter into a relationship with God that liberates us from the devil's deceptive, destructive rule and places us under God's sovereignty, his good and caring rule.

Because the Kingdom of God has come near enough for believers to see and enter it, Paul could honestly tell Christian slaves to obediently serve their earthly masters while recognizing at the same time, "It is the Lord Christ you are serving" (Col. 3:24). Daniel experienced a foretaste of this, even though he lived hundreds of years before Jesus came. When he and his friends landed in Babylon, they entered "the king's service" (Dan. 1:5). That is, they served the earthly king. And yet, as we have already seen, even the earthly king recognized that Daniel continually served a higher King (Dan. 6:16, 20). Like those slaves, you as a Christian there in your workplace, have the right and privilege to live under God's rule, even though outwardly someone else is running the show. To do so requires that you walk and work, not by what you see in the temporary power structure around you, but by faith in the Kingdom God himself has set up.

God's Kingdom Will Crush and End All Man-Made Kingdoms. The promise that God himself would someday set up a kingdom that would end all the others kept kingdom-of-Babylon matters in perspective for Daniel. Yes, his work for Babylon served to help carry out God's first command to rule the earth, and he did it wholeheartedly. But he did not see his work as the be-all and end-all of his life. Suppose you own a home that stands in the path of a freeway the government plans to build. Working through the courts, the government condemns your house and announces plans to bulldoze it in three years. Until then, you may rent it out. How much money will you invest to improve your lame-duck house? You'll spend some money to replace burned out light bulbs and fix leaky toilets. But you won't add any rooms or install granite countertops. Instead, you'll invest in ways that will pay off in your new and permanent home. Knowing the kingdom of God will do away with all earthly power structures will shape how you invest your time, effort and money.

In his book, *The Heavenly Good of Earthly Work*, Darrell Cosden writes, "When we do not seek the future in God, we end up looking for hope elsewhere—and our built-in human longings for a future, growth, and progress will compel us to try to create utopia for ourselves. . . . But without God and his kingdom in focus, all of our visions of what this future should look like become misdirected and are bound to go wrong. And if theology alone were not enough to convince us, the last couple of centuries of world history prove that we are not very good at creating heaven without God through our work and technology." God's coming kingdom will eliminate and replace all earthly kingdoms. Knowing that will motivate you to shape your work time and effort in light of that eternal kingdom.

God's Kingdom Will Last Forever. This promise freed Daniel from building his life on the shimmering soap-bubble of the kingdom of Babylon—which burst after only 53 years. His peers engaged in political plots and intrigues in their desperate pursuit to gain places in that temporary kingdom. His faith in God's eternal kingdom relieved Daniel of all such pressure. You and I have that same promise. But we have something even better. Because God's kingdom has come near in the One who said that this kingdom is within us (Lk. 17:21), we can begin enjoying its never-ending benefits now.

Consider how things appear where you work. In Satan's temporary kingdom, he promises that its power, wealth and knowledge will bring fulfillment, security and happiness. He promotes the lie that this life is all there is. That you should get all you can now, because when it's over, it's all done. So sacrifice everything to get that position of influence while you still can. Double your income, even if you have to neglect your family. Push on to get another degree so you can compete for the highest rung on the success ladder. Such lies lead to dead ends.

But once you're under the rule of the God who tells you the truth, you begin to shape your life around his *forever* promises. "He who feeds on this bread will live *forever*" (Jn. 6:58). "He [God the Father] will give you another comforter who will be with you *forever*" (Jn. 14:16). We who enter God's kingdom will receive "a crown that will last *forever*" (I Cor. 9:25). We will "be with the Lord *forever*" (I Thess. 4:17). And we have the promise that "the man who does the will of God lives *forever*" (I Jn. 2:17). [Italics added for emphasis.] When through the cross of Christ you enter the kingdom that will last forever, the compulsion to work obsessively to get it all now loses its steam.

God's Kingdom Will be Ruled By Jesus. Daniel did not yet know the coming ruler by the name "Jesus." But he saw that the Most High God, the "Ancient of Days," would give the eternal kingdom-authority to "one like a son of man" (Dan. 7:13-14). Even so, people all over the world would "worship" him. This may have puzzled Daniel. Worship belongs only to God. How, then, could this ruler who would be "like a son of man" [human] be rightfully worshiped? Although Daniel could not have known the details, we now know that this prophecy perfectly fits Jesus, the Word-who-was-God who became flesh and lived among us.

Throughout history the rulers of this world's kingdoms have seized and maintained their power through violence, war and killing. Nebuchadnezzar would have ordered the deaths of all his wise men just because they could not read his mind. From Alexander the Great to Adolf Hitler and from Stalin to Saddam Hussein, the list is long of the rulers who established their kingdoms through bloodshed. The sovereignty over the kingdom of God also came to Jesus through bloodshed—but the blood was his own. Because Jesus "became obedient to death—even death on a cross . . . God exalted him to the highest place and gave him the name that is above every name, that at the name of Jesus every knee should bow, in heaven and on earth and under the earth, and every tongue confess that Jesus Christ is Lord, to the glory of God the Father" (Phil. 2:8-11).

What a contrast to the self-serving rulers in the litter-box of world history! Daniel worked for some of those world-rulers. But he lived and waited for the eternal kingdom to be ruled by the "one like a son of man." Daniel held positions of great authority in a world-kingdom. Yet he did not lust after power. The prospect of the kingdom coming insulated him from the high voltage of selfish ambition. He remained a servant throughout his government career.

We who live in light of the cross know that God's coming kingdom will be ruled not by power-hungry politicians and bloodthirsty conquerors. Instead, the One who sacrificed himself for the life of the world will head it up. John the apostle saw how the transition to this kingdom will take place: "The seventh angel sounded his trumpet, and there were loud voices in heaven, which said: 'The kingdom of the world has become the kingdom of our Lord and of his Christ, and he will reign for ever and ever'" (Rev. 11:15). Knowing that the coming kingdom will be ruled by the self-sacrificing Jesus should transform the way you approach your work. In him, you see that true greatness, real authority, belongs not to the manipulator, not to the political pusher and shover, but to the one who lays down his life for others. Knowing that "Jesus shall reign where e'er the sun doth his successive journeys run," you can display his spirit of servant-greatness even there in your workplace.

God's Kingdom Will be Given to His People. In chapter 7, Daniel repeatedly hears the kingdom-inheritance theme in the interpretation of his dream. Verse 18: "But the saints of the Most

High will receive the kingdom and possess it forever." Verse 22: ". . . the Ancient of Days came and pronounced judgment in favor of the saints of the Most High, and the time came when they possessed the kingdom." Verse 27: "Then the sovereignty, power and greatness of the kingdoms under the whole heaven will be handed over to the saints, the people of the Most High."

This fits perfectly with what Jesus would later tell his disciples: ". . . your Father has been pleased to give you the kingdom" (Lk. 12:32). And it fits what both Paul and James in the New Testament say about inheriting the kingdom and about our being God's "heirs." If you are convinced Jesus Christ will include you in the government of his coming eternal kingdom, it will put your work here in this world into perspective. The very last words Daniel heard from the messenger sent from God assured him that he would rise to receive his "allotted inheritance" (12:13). What a fitting final word for this man who did not let the kingdom of Babylon corrupt him because he waited patiently for the kingdom of God.

But the promise of this allotted inheritance belongs to you as a Christ-follower just as much as it did to Daniel. The New Testament writers consistently say so. James assures us that God has "chosen those who are poor in the eyes of the world to be rich in faith and to inherit the kingdom he promised those who love him" (Jas. 2:5). Paul appeals to our inheritance as a motive for doing ordinary work: "Whatever you do, work at it with all your heart, as working for the Lord, not for men, since you know that you will receive an inheritance from the Lord as a reward" (Col. 3:23-24). God's Word cannot fail. As you do your daily work, you can be certain that you are guaranteed a share in exercising authority in God's Kingdom. You don't have to elbow your way to a place of significance or influence in this short life. Your place will be given to you as a gift in the kingdom that is coming.

So what practical value does a kingdom-of-God vision, based on his promises, have in your workplace? It will cut the legs from under worry and workaholism. It will deliver you from using your work to pursue the endless maze of utopian rabbit trails. It will outshine and override the dazzling, mesmerizing power, wealth and wisdom of this world. It will empower you to seek greatness through servanthood. And it will release you from the struggle for a significant place in this temporary kingdom, because God has already guaranteed your place in his coming Kingdom.

Only kingdom-of-God vision can sustain any real ministry in the workplace. Sadly, our Christian subculture has taught us to think in church terms instead of Kingdom terms. Reggie McNeal, in *Missional Renaissance*, calls for a shift from church-based back to kingdom-based leadership. He points out that Christian leaders in the New Testament "weren't consumed with building and operating the church as an institution." Instead, they "did whatever they did, whether preaching or pastoral care or whatever, for the sake of the kingdom movement." But as the centuries rolled by, "The biblical idea that followers of Jesus are called to live out his mission in the world became replaced by the substitute agenda of church members expressing their religious devotion through church activities superintended by the clergy."

What role does the church play in relationship to the kingdom of God? An Old Testament incident may help to clarify the church's responsibility. In 930 B.C., the kingdom of Israel split into two kingdoms—Judah in the south and Israel to the north. Nearly 100 years later, Elisha commissioned a young prophet to anoint Jehu as the eleventh king of the northern kingdom of Israel. The prophet poured oil on Jehu's head and pronounced God's words, "I anoint you king over the Lord's people Israel." Through those words, Jehu received the God-given authority to rule—the essence of a kingdom. When Jehu told the men with him what the prophet had said, they blew a trumpet and shouted, "Jehu is king!" (II Kgs. 9:6, 13).

Jehu's authority pictures the *kingdom of God*—Christ's God-given authority to rule over all. The men who publicly declared

Jehu's kingship illustrate the role of the *church*—to announce the coming of God's kingdom in the Person of King Jesus. Jehu's men pointed not to themselves but to their king—just as the church is not to call attention to itself but to its King. Jehu's men did not arrange to pursue their own agenda, nor should the church develop a script of its own. However many men were with Jehu, none set up his own shop to promote his own private take on the kingdom. Instead, they all joined forces to make the new king known to everyone—just as the church is called to do. By the way we speak and live and love, we the church are to make it plain that Jesus is Lord over the kingdom of God now here and yet to come.

Kingdom Vision Versus Church Vision.

In his book, *The Other Six Days*, R. Paul Stevens writes: "Kingdom ministry has been almost totally eclipsed by church ministry. Ministry is viewed as advancing the church rather than the Kingdom." Other than fueling financial contributions, the workplace plays little or no role in the traditional church system. The church has no authority over the workplace or the people in its power structures. To a program-centered church, the workplace may even seem like a competitor—devouring hours that could otherwise be devoted to church projects. Traditional church-vision limits us to buildings and fixed addresses and denominations and religious programs. Kingdom-vision lets us see that Jesus, as sovereign King of all, rules not just in our church circles but everywhere.

As Daniel knew, God's Kingdom does have authority over the workplace and all those who exercise power within it. In Daniel's vision, ". . . the Most High God is sovereign over the kingdoms of men and sets over them anyone he wishes" (Dan. 5:21). The "kingdoms of men" include the corporations and companies that are run by authorities (whose power comes from God, even if they do not realize it). Daniel discovered that God was at work not only among the covenant people of Israel but even in the pagan kingdom of Babylon. Who else gave Nebuchadnezzar his dreams? Who gave this earthly king his power? Who shut the mouths of the lions? Who appeared in the Babylonian furnace? Who gave Daniel favor with the chief official? Whose hand wrote the cryptic message on the palace wall? No one else but the sovereign Creator-Sustainer God.

Our focus needs to shift from the (institutional) church to the kingdom. Richard Broholm wrote, "I slowly began to discover that Christ stands at the center of our life in the world where we expend most of our time and expertise. I found that he is, indeed, Lord of the world, albeit a suffering-servant Lord who redeems and reconciles the world through his apparent powerlessness on the cross." The "church world" can too easily become an isolating ghetto. Do you live in the church world, thinking that any significant work by and for God happens within that context? Or do you live in the Kingdom that has broken into the world and now invisibly permeates it everywhere without regard for artificial sacred/secular boundaries?

Our long tradition of church-focused vision can blind you to the connection between your career and God's kingdom. In the context of your workplace, what does it mean to seek God's kingdom first? Begin with the fact that the kingdom of God equals the rule of God. So on the job, seeking first his kingdom means making it your top priority to let him rule in your work life—your decisions, your relationships, your attitudes, your conversations, your work quality and everything else. Given your job and the people you work with, what would God have you to do? Many other forces in the work world—such as selfish ambition, greed, rivalry, or hunger for power—are constantly pressing to get you to put your own this-world-kingdom interests first.

An analogy may help you see the link between God's kingdom and your workplace. In some ways, your role resembles that of an ambassador and your job compares with an embassy. In II Cor. 5:20 Paul speaks of being "ambassadors for Christ." In the United States, an ambassador gets assigned to an embassy in a country with which our government has set up a diplomatic relationship. During Jesus' time on earth, he ended the enmity that had blocked citizens of the world's kingdom from entering the kingdom of God. You might say in Christ God created a "diplomatic relationship" through which former enemies of God can now approach him.

Within a foreign country, the building housing a U. S. embassy and the land it sits on still belong to the host country. But the U.S. ambassador has the say-so over what goes on inside the building. Similarly, your job belongs to your employer, but because you occupy the job, you have a measure of control over how you do your work. As a U.S. citizen, the ambassador is still subject to the U.S. Constitution and laws. But he or she also conforms to the laws of the host country. For example, the ambassador to New Zealand would observe that nation's customs and laws by driving on the left side of the road. As a citizen of the kingdom of God, you obey King Jesus. But you also comply with all the rules and practices of your company, unless doing so would cause you to disobey him.

A U.S. ambassador in, say, Italy doesn't go there simply to enjoy great pasta. Instead, his or her mission there is to represent the interests of the U.S. If a question arises about the U.S. policy on foreign trade, the prime minister of Italy can get a reliable answer from the U.S. ambassador. If it becomes important for the U.S. to communicate something to the Italian government, the U.S. president may send that word through the U.S. ambassador. As an ambassador of the kingdom of God with a job inside the kingdom of this world, you represent King Jesus. Those in your workplace should be able to look to you for authentic glimpses of what God is like and what it means to live life as a citizen of his kingdom.

The U.S. ambassador in France also serves other Americans who happen to be living in that country. A tourist runs out of money; the embassy helps her contact people back home who can wire funds. After a traffic accident in Paris, the injured Americans need medical attention; the embassy helps them locate doctors, hospitals and clinics and notifies the family back home. A couple from Denver gives birth to a baby while visiting relatives in France; the embassy receives their report of birth abroad to document the infant's U.S. citizenship and obtains a passport for the newborn. In a similar way, one of the reasons God has placed you in your job as an "ambassador" is to serve other believers in your work circles. We'll take a deeper look at how to do so in Chapter Seven.

Growing up on a cultivated truck farm, I was delighted when Dad—behind schedule in spring soil preparation—let me skip school to drive tractor. At first, I tried to drive a straight line by watching one of the front tires. This shortsighted vision always left zigs and zags in my wake. So Dad taught me another way to drive. "Lift your eyes," he said. "Pick out a spot on that distant mountain. Point the radiator cap at that spot. Then keep aiming for it as you drive through the field." I did. And once I practiced that higher vision, the paths behind me became ruler-straight. Like the wheels on a tractor, the church Jesus promised to build plays an important role. But focusing on church "wheels" will not help you steer a straight course in your workplace. Instead, raise your sights to the "mountain," to the coming kingdom and to its King.

Only with a vision of the kingdom of God—the panoramic picture—will you keep things in true perspective as you work in this world. But you need to bring another picture, a much smaller one, into focus as well: your own identity as a follower of Christ. Daniel knew who he was, as we'll see in chapter three.

Putting It to Work

- In what ways has the work world's promises of power, wealth or knowledge affected your priorities as a Christian?
- This chapter quotes George Eldon Ladd on the biblical definition of a kingdom. How might this definition differ from the way you have understood the term?

- Daniel's dream interpretations included five kingdom promises. Choose the promise that seems most relevant to your job—and explain why you selected it.
- Describe how a kingdom-of-God perspective would differ from a my-church perspective in terms of their influence on the believer in the workplace.
- List three ways seeking God's kingdom first would profoundly shape the way you approach your daily work.

CHAPTER THREE

IDENTITY: KNOWING WHO YOU ARE

"But you are a chosen people, a royal priesthood, a holy nation, a people belonging to God, that you may declare the praises of him who called you out of darkness into his wonderful light."
I Pet. 2:9

"God made us who we are to show the world who he is."
John Piper, "Christian Identity and Christian Destiny"

Framing the Issue: After years in the world of work, many people let their jobs or their titles define them. As a Christian in so-called "secular" work, you can lose also sight of your true identity by buying into man-made religious traditions. Daniel never caved in to efforts to change his real identity. Knowing who he was stabilized him through all the ups and downs of his career.

How could Daniel and Henry Hill have anything in common?

Henry Hill's criminal history had put him on the wrong side of the mob. So in 1980, to avoid getting murdered by the Mafia or locked up by the law, Henry entered the U.S. Marshal's Witness Protection Program, along with his wife and their two children. In exchange for this protection, Henry agreed to testify against his former crime companions. His testimony helped convict 50 underworld characters. In 2004 his children, Gregg and Gina, told their story in a book, *On the Run: a Mafia Childhood.*

WITSEC, the Witness Security Program run by the U. S. Marshals Service, has protected around 500 witnesses and their families a year since it began in 1970. In its official website, the U. S. Marshals Service describes what typically happens after it admits a witness into the program: ". . . the procedure usually involves the immediate removal of the witness and his/her immediate family members from the danger area and their relocation to a secure area selected by the Marshals Service. Witnesses and their families typically get new identities with authentic documentation. Housing, medical care, job training and employment can also be provided. Subsistence funding to cover basic living expenses is also provided to the witnesses until they become self-sufficient in the relocation area."

WITSEC aims to accomplish something completely different with its witnesses than what King Nebuchadnezzar had in mind for Daniel. But much of what happens to a protected witness today happened to Daniel back then. The witness is relocated; so was Daniel. WITSEC helps the witness find a new job; Nebuchadnezzar found one for Daniel. And the witness receives a new name; as did Daniel. Through these drastic changes, the U. S. Marshalls Service seeks to erase the original identity of the witness so that he or she may survive to testify in court. Nebuchadnezzar wanted to erase Daniel's original identity so that he would live, think, act and work as a loyal Babylonian.

Daniel: Aware of His Own Identity.

Daniel arrived in Babylon knowing who he was. From toddler-hood he had known himself as "Daniel," which means "God is my Judge." In *The NIV Application Commentary*, Tremper Longman III notes that in our Western culture, "name and identity are only mildly associated. In the ancient Near East, however, the name, which often contained the name of one's deity, was integrally connected with a person's identity." The "-el" in the name Daniel, was the most common Semitic word for deity—often combining with other descriptions of the true God: *Elohim, Eloah, El Shaddai* and so on. So from earliest childhood, Daniel had known himself as one answerable to the God who had revealed himself throughout the history of his people, the Israelites.

But after Daniel came to Babylon, King Nebuchadnezzar as-signed him a new name: Belteshazzar. Many believe this name meant, "Bel protect his life." Whatever the actual meaning, the first three letters of the new name referred to Bel Marduk, the top-ranking god of the city of Babylon and the empire of Babylonia. Nebuchadnezzar himself explained that he named Daniel Belteshazzar, "after the name of my god" (Dan. 4:8). Bel came from the word *baal,* meaning lord. The false god Baal appears throughout the Old Testament. For example, the wicked Ahab, king of Israel, "set up an altar for Baal in the temple of Baal that he built in Samaria" (I Kgs. 16:32).

So in addition to a new country and a new job, Nebuchadnezzar foisted on Daniel a new name, a name meant to wipe out his old identity and replace it with a new one. Not once does the Bible even hint that Daniel objected to having the Babylonians refer to him as Belteshazzar. His attitude seems to have been, "Call me whatever you wish."

But it's clear that the new name did nothing to change the way Daniel saw himself. We know the book that bears his name by Daniel, not by Belteshazzar. Nine times after the Babylonians renamed him Belteshazzar, Daniel refers to himself as, "I, Daniel . . ." (7:15, 28; 8:1, 15, 27; 9:2; 10:2, 7; and 12:5). So in Daniel's own heart and mind, his original identity remained intact. He was "God is my Judge." His relationship to the true God defined who he was—and he knew it from the beginning to the end of his career in Babylon. Knowing his identity helped Daniel remain steady through one on-the-job test after another.

Staying Pure. In Chapter One, he faces the food test. His reason for declining what comes from the king's kitchen had nothing to do with following a weight-loss diet, being a vegan, or allergies to wheat gluten. Instead, he turns the menu down because it will "defile" him. It will make him unfit for close fellowship with God. God is his judge. Not the chef. Not his peers. He decides what to do on the basis of who he knows himself to be in relationship to God.

Under Threat. In Chapter Two, Daniel learns of the king's decree that all his advisors will die because none can tell him his dream. When the king of Babylon makes up his mind to execute his top-level staff, no one on earth has the power to trump his order. But Daniel is not intimidated. Nebuchadnezzar is not his judge. God is. So, in effect, Daniel and his friends take their appeal to the Supreme Court of heaven. Because God is his Judge, Daniel knows God will hear him when he presents his case.

Speaking Unwanted Truth. In Chapter Four, Daniel listens with mounting horror as his employer relates his latest dream. The dream involved a fruit tree so tall it seemed to reach the clouds. It provided food for everyone, shelter for animals and a home for birds. Then, abruptly, a heavenly voice ordered it cut down, its branches lopped off, its leaves stripped and its fruit scattered. Nothing but its stump—bound with iron and bronze—would remain in the ground. As the interpretation dawns on him, Daniel must be turning white, because his boss tells him, "do not let the dream or its meaning alarm you." Knowing who he is, knowing God is his Judge, Daniel speaks boldly—not with a fleshly boldness, but with a confidence in God and God's acceptance of him as a messenger. With great courage, he tells the head of the world's greatest superpower the horrible news: You're about to be driven from office, turned into a virtual animal, eat grass and live outdoors like a cow. This will continue "until you learn that the Most High is sovereign over the kingdoms of men and gives it to anyone he wishes." The employee speaking this way to his boss is Daniel, the man who knows that "God [not Nebuchadnezzar] is my Judge."

Taking Demotion. In Chapter Five, another boss has taken over. Although Daniel remains in Babylon, the new king hasn't even heard of him. So when a thousand of the king's grand pooh-bahs, wives and concubines gather for a drinking bash, Daniel isn't there. He hasn't even been invited. Suddenly the disembodied fingers of a human hand write a cryptic message on the plaster wall. The king's legs turn rubbery. Can anyone interpret the strange markings? No one can. As the rest of the blood drains from the king's face, the queen informs him of Daniel and his god-like interpretive abilities.

So the king summons Daniel and promises him instant promotion. Although he is now a "nobody," Daniel is not impressed. "You may keep your gifts for yourself and give your rewards to someone else. Nevertheless, I will read the writing for the king and tell him what it means." And once again, Daniel tells the unwanted truth to the face of a powerful executive. His ups and downs in terms of official rank in the kingdom of Babylon do not change him at all. He still has confidence in God's ability to reveal the interpretations of baffling mysteries—and of his own place before God to be his instrument. Worldly rank (or the lack of it) means nothing to Daniel, because he knows who he is. Ultimately, he answers only to God.

Surviving Office Politics. In Chapter Six, the Babylonian kingdom has been conquered by the Medes and Persians. So Daniel serves under a new king. He does his work so well, the king wants to put him in charge of all his under-secretaries. These envious rivals, finding nothing to criticize in Daniel's work, concoct a scheme to be rid of him (covered in more detail in Chapter Six). But their devious plans don't ruffle Daniel. He is not answerable to those ambitious co-workers or to an unjust law. He is Daniel. "God is my judge." If wrong, God will judge him so. If not, the Judge of all the earth, the God who created lions, can certainly send angelic help.

Daniel's self-identity, anchored in his relationship to God, points forward to the self-concept we see in the Lord Jesus Christ. Although aware of his deity ("Before Abraham was, I Am."), Jesus the Man identified himself in terms of his relationship with God the Father. "I and the Father are one" (Jn. 10:30). When asked, "Are you then the Son of God?" he answered, "You are right in saying I am" (Lk. 22:70). And in praying for his followers, he asked, ". . . that all of them may be one, Father, just as you are in me and I am in you" (Jn. 17:21).

Further, the effort to erase Daniel's identity self-concept reflects a similar attempt to undermine Jesus' identity. At the beginning of Jesus' public ministry, Satan began the first two wilderness temptations with the almost sneering words, "If you are the Son of God . . ." (Mt. 4:3, 6). In other words, are you really so sure of who you claim to be? If so, then prove it. And as Jesus hung on the cross, Satan's human mouthpieces would later challenge his identity as well: "Come down from the cross, if you are the Son of God!" (Mt. 27:40). Between the wilderness and the cross, others joined the effort to erase Jesus' real identity: ". . . you, a mere man, claim to be God" (Jn. 10:33).

Today's Assault on the Believer's Identity.

In light of the attempts on the self-identity of both Daniel and Jesus, it should come as no surprise that a similar effort is being waged to sabotage the identity of believers today. In his book,

The Jesus Way, Eugene Peterson calls this effort "a barefaced lie, insinuated into the Christian community by the devil." What's the lie? Peterson says, "Within the Christian community there are few words that are more disabling than 'layperson' and 'laity.' The words convey the impression—an impression that quickly solidifies into a lie—that there is a two-level hierarchy among the men and women who follow Jesus. . . . It is a lie because it misleads a huge company of Christians into assuming that their workplace severely limits their usefulness in the cause of Christ, that it necessarily confines them to part-time work for Jesus as they help out on the margins of kingdom work."

In his seminar, Resurrection Friends, Peterson said, "The devil does some of his best work when he gets Christians to think of themselves as Christian laypersons." Peterson is not alone in seeing the crippling effect this *layperson* identity exerts within the body of Christ.

- Lesslie Newbigin wrote that the word layman "has come to mean, in common speech, an ignoramus, an outsider."
- John Stott: "'Lay' is often a synonym for 'amateur' as opposed to 'professional,' or 'unqualified' as opposed to 'expert.' "
- R. Paul Stevens: "'Only a layperson' is a phrase that must never be found on our lips. It is irreverent and demeaning."

And yet, conditioned by centuries of church tradition, countless believers think of themselves in these terms that Peterson calls "disabling" and Stevens calls "demeaning." For example, a woman who hosts a TV talk show that explores the Christian lifestyle within American culture says of herself: "I'm not a minister, I'm just a layperson."

The following quotations from Internet blogs and responses to them suggest how widespread this self-concept has become:

- "I'm just a layperson, not a pastor or church leader."
- "I wouldn't know, since I'm just a layperson."
- "I'm just a layperson, looking from the sidelines."
- "I'm not a Biblical scholar, by any means, just a 'layperson,' so some of the insights I have in this blog will be… 'inaccurate,' for lack of a better term."
- "If you are a Christian—a Pastor or just a layperson, I urge you to watch this video."

Two of the three words in this recurring phrase, so common in Christian lingo, work to erase the real identity of Christian believers: the word "just" and the word "layperson." (The "a" in the middle seems harmless.)

In every one of the five quotations just bulleted, the "just" means merely. It conveys insignificance, unimportance, triviality or slightness. If you notice a kitten's claw-mark on my arm and cluck your tongue, I might answer: "It's just a scratch." In other words, it's nothing serious. If your four-year-old awakens in a panic after a nightmare, you're likely to calm her by saying, "It was just a dream." It had no real substance. We use the *just* word to minimize all kinds of things. It was just a joke. Just a drop. Just a theory. Just a piece of paper. Scripture never distinguishes among believers to classify some as insignificant or unimportant.

In each quotation, the "just" joins forces with that demeaning, disabling word, "layperson." Yes, it admits, you're a person, but merely a *lay*person. You have less to offer than a *clergy*person. How did the English words "lay" and "laity" worm their way into the vocabulary of Christians? They did *not* come directly from the biblical word "laos," the Greek word which simply means people. Laos appears 142 times in the Greek New Testament. And whenever it refers to Christians, it includes all of us without distinction. For example God, in describing the New Covenant relationships, says, "I will be their God, and they will be my people [laos]" (Heb. 8:10). Obviously the *laos* of God wraps in every believer apart from any thought of rank or status—the baby one, the mature one, the slave, the evangelist, and so on.

The way we use the words "lay" and "laity" comes not from *laos* but from *laikos*. *Laikos* means "of the common people." So this word divides us into two groups—the common and the uncommon people. New Testament writers never use the word *laikos*. The first Christian writer to use that term was Clement of Rome around the year 96 A.D. After identifying church roles of high priest, priests and Levites (all Old Covenant titles), Clement wrote that, "The layman [*laikos*] is bound by the laws that pertain to laymen." In other Greek literature, *laikos* was a synonym for *idiotes* (from which we get our word idiot).

Clement and others veered from the New Testament *laos* and adopted *laikos* to mean the common people. This created the need for another word to describe the uncommon people. Thus the word *clergy* came into use as early as the third century A. D. The roots of *clergy* go indirectly back to another New Testament word, *kleros*. *Kleros* means lot or inheritance or share. When the New Testament uses kleros to describe God's people, it includes all of us. For example, I Pet. 5:3 speaks of the whole church as God's heritage or inheritance (*kleros*). But *klerikos,* used nowhere in the New Testament, came to refer just to those "ordained to perform pastoral or sacerdotal [sacred] functions in a Christian church" (Merriam-Webster Online Dictionary).

What has resulted from all this verbal sleight-of-hand? Countless believers have lost sight of who they really are. Like those in the witness protection program, they have had their true identities erased and have come to see themselves as "just laypersons." Imagine the Christian teacher or computer programmer, whose co-worker asks a question about his or her faith, answering: "I wouldn't know, since I'm just a layperson." A completely unbiblical response.

Suppose Nebuchadnezzar had been curious after hearing Daniel say that "the God of heaven will set up a kingdom" (2:44). What if the king had asked, "How is this 'God of heaven' different from Bel Marduk?" Imagine Daniel responding by saying, "I wouldn't know. You see, I'm just a layperson." Daniel, of course, not influenced by the centuries of church tradition that now color our thinking, would not have responded with such a self put-down. But what else can we expect of a Christian today who has been sold an unbiblical identity?

Who are you according to the man-made teachings of Christendom? You are *just a layperson* (this has not one shred of support in the New Testament).

How does this *just-a-layperson* identity insinuate itself into your work? It will shrink-wrap your imagination with all kinds of ministry-shriveling thoughts: *You are unqualified to deal with your co-workers in spiritual ministry; leave that role in the hands of the clergy. You're an amateur. Many of your insights will be inaccurate. Don't even bother taking steps to improve your skills as a workplace minister; that's just not who you are.*

But no. As a Christian living in the age of God's grace and his outpoured Holy Spirit, what is your God-given identity? Who does God say you are in his written Word? The New Testament leaves no doubt that God wants you to know who you really are. In fact, he has provided a number of picture-words to bring your true self-concept into focus. Let's look at just a few of them—along with what they mean for you in your workplace.

You are a *priest* (I Pet. 2:5-9; Rev. 5:9, 10). As a priest, you stand before God on behalf of co-workers by praying for them. You also represent God to them as you show them, by your work and your words, what God is like. As we saw in chapter two, God has sent you into your workplace as his ambassador.

You are *salt* (Matt. 5:13). As one of God's salty people, you permeate your workplace to create thirst in co-workers, to retard decay and to bring out the real flavor of life as God means it to be.

You are *light* (Matt. 5:14). You illuminate pockets of darkness so that those around you may see things not as they imagine them but as they really are. In you, goodness, righteousness and truth, which Paul calls the "fruit of the light" (Eph. 5:9), become not abstractions but behaviors others can observe.

You are seed (Matt. 13:38). Like a kernel of wheat, you carry the germ of a Life that can take root in co-workers, grow and bear fruit. God has scattered his kingdom people all over the earth. You, as a seed, have landed in the unique soil of your particular workplace.

You are a *temple* (I Cor. 6:19). You house God. When you show up in your workplace, you offer God a center—your body—from which he can work. Offering God the temple of your body, as Paul says in Rom. 12:1, is a "spiritual act of worship." If co-workers come into your work space, they enter a zone where the everywhere-present God lives in a special way.

You are a *branch of the Christ-Vine* (Jn. 15:5). The fruit of God's Spirit—love, joy, peace, patience, kindness, goodness, faithfulness, gentleness and self-control—is attractive enough to whet the appetite even of unbelievers. But those desirable qualities can seem to them hopelessly out of reach. As a branch, you bring this seed-bearing fruit to a level where hungry co-workers can grasp it.

You are a child of God (Jn. 1:12). Right there on the job, by the way you speak, react and do your work, you can show the family likeness of God. God is love. As one of the Father's children, you remind others of him as you love his other children. As you respond with compassion to those still in the grip of sin. And as you bless even his enemies.

You are a *part of Christ's body* (I Cor. 12:27). Through your God-given gifts, you are equipped to serve and encourage others throughout the week—and not just in official gatherings of believers.

The list could go on. But these at least illustrate who you really are in Christ. Daniel never let go of his God-given identity—in spite of pressures designed to erase it and replace it with a false one. Let Daniel's example inspire you. Refuse to think of yourself or any other believer with those put-down words, "just a layperson." That label has sprung from human religious traditions which Jesus said nullify the Word of God (Matt. 15:6).

The musical version of Victor Hugo's *Les Miserables* beautifully illustrates the life-changing power of God-given identity. Valjean, imprisoned 19 years for stealing a loaf of bread to feed a starving child, has just been paroled. The song that opens the musical captures the self-concept he and the other prisoners have been conditioned to believe: "Look down, look down, you'll always be a slave." As the policeman Javert informs Valjean of his parole, he reminds him of who he is: "You are a thief. . . . You robbed a house." Later, the lawman tells Valjean, "A man like you can never change."

Unable as a parolee to find work or food or lodging, Valjean nearly gives up. But an old priest takes pity on him and invites him in to spend the night. Living up to what he has been told he is, Valjean steals the priest's silver table service and slips out before dawn. The police nab him and take him to the priest to return the silver. But the priest acts as if he had given the silver to Valjean—and insists that his guest forgot to take the matching candle holders. Then, after dismissing the police officers, the priest says to Valjean: "And remember this, my brother, see in this some higher plan. You must use this precious silver to become an honest man. By the witness of the martyrs, by the Passion and the Blood, God has raised you out of darkness. I have bought your soul for God!" The priest's act of grace rocks Valjean to the core. And in his reflection on what has just happened, he recalls, "He called me Brother." Agonizingly, he leaves behind his old identity: "Jean Val jean is nothing now. Another story must begin." As the musical continues, that other story becomes obvious in the life of the former convict's new identity.

Train yourself to think of who you are in biblical ways—even while immersed in your everyday work. As a believer in Jesus Christ, you are a priest, salt, light, seed and so on *not* because you feel that way, but because God says that's who you are. So this matter of your identity in the workplace requires from you, as it did from Daniel, an exercise of faith. And that will allow for "another story" to begin in the way you approach your daily work.

Understanding more and more who you are in Christ has a flip side: recognizing who you're *not*. Co-workers will promote ideas and practices that would undermine the real you. Although the work world is your assignment, it's not your address. Your life is hidden with Christ in God. That's where you live. So, like Daniel, you'll need to practice a detachment that avoids distance, a separation that is not standoffish. Chapter four will explore how Daniel did just that.

PUTTING IT TO WORK

- Identify some ways you think the working-world system has influenced your own understanding of your identity. (For example, the world labels you as a "consumer.")
- Look back over the time you've spent in Christian circles. What experiences or teachings might have contributed to an unbiblical self-identity? Be specific.
- Have you ever used the self-put-down, "I'm just a layperson"? If so, illustrate with an actual example.
- This chapter lists eight terms from the New Testament that describe your identity as a follower of Christ (Priest. Salt. Light. Seed. Temple. Branch of the Christ-Vine. Child of God. Part of Christ's body.) Which of these have you already made part of the way you view of yourself at work? Which might you yet need to incorporate?
- How would it change your approach to your work if you thought of yourself in these eight ways?
- Those eight are just a partial list of how the Bible describes your identity as a believer. What other biblical terms tell you who you are?

CHAPTER FOUR

SEPARATION: DETACHING THE HEART

"Religion that God our Father accepts as pure and faultless is this: to look after orphans and widows in their distress and to keep oneself from being polluted by the world."
    Jas. 1:27

"Over the centuries, Christians have had varying responses to the secular marketplace. Some, like the Amish, attempt to isolate themselves from the corrupting influence of the secular world. . . . In recent years the trend has been for Christians to segregate their spiritual church life from their secular work life. This attitude allows many to believe they can conform to the compromised values of our culture without impacting the spiritual aspects of their life."
    Steve Cable, Probe Ministries

Framing the Issue: Some Christians will warn you to keep your distance from the work world. So Christians have retreated from all kinds of fields—public education, law, politics and the media, to name just a few. Young Daniel plunged into a world full of temptation. Fully in it, yes. Yet because he exercised spiritual strategy, he remained uncontaminated by its poisons and free of its traps.

Daniel didn't just happen into "secular" work. God sent him there. A vision of God's Kingdom sustained Daniel decade after decade in his career. Knowing his true identity worked within him like a stabilizing gyroscope. But none of these God-given gifts spared him from colliding with the unholy moral atmosphere of his workplace. By "moral atmosphere," I mean the commonly accepted values and behavior of the peers, supervisors and subordinates around him.

What describes the climate where you work? Do you sometimes feel you're in thick spiritual smog? Co-workers avoid Jesus' name except as a swear word. Gossip and back-stabbing never stop. Pressures to compete lead to lying or cheating. Off-color jokes and stories multiply during coffee breaks and lunch hours. Diversity training pushes values you know to be worthless. The ladders to more money and power seem like shortcuts to fulfillment and security. If your job puts you in an atmosphere like that, what are you as a Christian to do?

Many in Christian circles—even some church leaders—are calling for believers to retreat from the "dirty" world of work. Here are some recent examples:

- From an article about a well known Christian university: *". . . after they've gone through the curriculum, many emerge more convinced than ever that journalism is no place for Christians."*
- From a message by a Christian pastor: *"The workplace is no place for a Christian woman. It is too hard to be spiritual there. . . . Stay out of the world!"*
- From a former soldier: *"I soon found that the military was really no place for a Christian. Daily my ears were assaulted with profane and obscene language . . . ."*
- From a Christian blogger: *"A graphic designer friend of mine was once told by well-meaning folks in church that he should not be involved in three types of jobs: an artist (due to wide-*

spread worldly temptation), a politician (because it's 'dirty')
or a lawyer (to avoid the lure of wealth)."

From these few examples you catch the drift of this point of
view: *Working out there in that corrupt world is hazardous to your*
spiritual health. So don't go there. But is God behind teaching like
that? Are we to pull out? To isolate ourselves? To hold our noses
till Jesus comes? What did Daniel do? How did he withstand un-
godliness in his workplace? And how does his example square
with our instructions from Jesus and his New Testament apostles?

An Ungodly Working Environment.

Daniel and his Jewish buddies have been transplanted from
the Holy Land to an unholy land. Instead of receiving lessons in
the Jewish Scriptures, they get assigned to study "the language
and literature of the Babylonians" (Dan. 1:4). According to Old
Testament professor Tremper Longman III, "Daniel clearly would
have been trained in the arts of divination [the use of omens to
foresee the future] through such means as interpreting unusual
celestial phenomena, astrology, the examination of sheep livers,
and so forth." By means of such training, their pagan king hopes
to make them forget their spiritual heritage and adopt their new
and worldly culture.

The name-changes noted in the previous chapter also reflect
the spiritually polluted environment. And yes, there's more. We
know from the 90-foot-tall image of gold in chapter 3 that Daniel's
co-workers had no qualms about worshiping idols. In Daniel 5
we see them indulging in wild drinking parties. Arrogance, not
humility, ruled (5:22-23). Over in 6:1-9 it's clear that intrigue,
conspiracy and deceit were all part of office politics. In other
words, the moral atmosphere in Daniel's workplace was just as
grimy as it often is today. Daniel's workplace immersed him in a
climate that clashed with his faith in the true God

A Workplace Full of Spiritual Hazards.

Daniel and his friends go through the weird training. They even put up with the name-changes. I might have drawn the line in the sand over the seminars on sheep livers—but apparently they do not. Then along comes the food issue. As 1:5 says, "The king assigned them a daily amount of food and wine from the king's table." But Daniel "resolved not to defile himself with the royal food and wine" (v. 8). Maybe some of the food from the king's kitchen is unclean by the standards of the Law God had given through Moses. Pork chops, for example, would have been off-limits for a kosher Israelite like Daniel. Or perhaps the food and wine has first been offered to one of the Babylonian false gods. Whatever the reason, eating it will violate Daniel's conscience. Even the food his employer provides is laced with spiritual arsenic.

Let's not kid ourselves. Working in the world does put you at spiritual risk. Today, under the New Covenant, we don't face the same food issues Daniel did. But for him, under the Old Covenant, eating entrees from the king's menu would have been hazardous to his spiritual health. He would have been "defiled," dirtied, stained, polluted. This world has the power to do that—even to us Christians. That's why James 1:27 warns us to keep ourselves "from being polluted by the world."

John the apostle says "the whole world is under the control of the evil one" (I Jn. 5:19). In his book, *Love Not the World*, the Chinese Christian leader, Watchman Nee, warns us how widely Satan's ruling influence extends throughout the world-system: "Politics, education, literature, science, art, law, commerce, music—such are the things that constitute the *kosmos* [world], and these are the things that we meet daily." And in a further word on the business world, Nee says, "I can think of no sphere where the temptation to dishonest and corrupt dealing is so great as here." So yes, as a Christian in the workplace you face real and rampant spiritual risks.

Daniel's Defense Strategy.

Given the moral sewage in Daniel's workplace, what is a God-loving man like him to do? Shall he refuse to work in Babylon? As we've seen, some Christians today would pressure him to withdraw from the rotten work world. "How?" Daniel might have asked. "By refusing all food? Then the king would kill me, and yes I'd escape—as a corpse!" But had Daniel chosen an escape route, his pagan co-workers would never have seen the sovereignty of God through the magnifying lens of his work.

How does Daniel resist the risk without running away? What forces does he unleash against that which would contaminate him? In Dan. 1:8-14, we see his response. Daniel's wall of defense includes four levels: *knowledge, decisiveness, favor* and *strategy*.

- Level one: *knowledge*. Daniel has internalized Scripture well enough to know that eating the king's menu will pollute his relationship with God.
- Second, he acts on that knowledge with *decisiveness*. The NIV translation says he "resolved" (v. 8). The original Hebrew says he decided this issue in his heart. Daniel is not double-minded.
- Third, he has *favor*—God's gift of outside help. "Now God had caused the official to show favor and sympathy to Daniel" (v. 9). Yes, the sovereign God can incline even hearts that don't know him to show favor to his people.
- And fourth, Daniel resists contamination with an intelligent *strategy*. He proposes a plan—the ten-day test diet. Others can accept it. And it allows God opportunity to work. No ultimatums. No in-your-face, my-way-or-else spirit. Instead, Daniel's request leaves the guard free to make up his own mind what to do at the end of the ten days.

The Happy Result.

After the ten days, Daniel and his Jewish friends could be models for a health-food magazine. Their impressive appearance makes the guard and the chief official look good in the king's eyes. So the test diet becomes permanent. The Jewish guys pass their tests and the king finds them ten times better than anybody else on the royal staff. Now these young men who have dared to be different to serve the one true and sovereign God begin to catch the attention of those in their work world. And as their lives will later show, the true and sovereign God is active not just in their Holy Land, but even here in the moral confusion of Babylon's workplaces. Daniel's creative strategy accomplishes two things. First, it opens the way for him to obey God. Second, it demonstrates his love for his workplace neighbors and preserves a harmonious working relationship with them.

Daniel faced this food issue early in his career in the bureaucracy. Yet even after spending decade after decade in this environment, Daniel finished spiritually alive and well. Although surrounded by the lures of wealth and power, he remained detached from them. For example, when King Belteshazzar offered him gold and glory if he would interpret what the hand wrote on the wall, Daniel shrugged the offer off: "You may keep your gifts for yourself and give your rewards to someone else" (5:17). What was his secret of separation? Today some Christians seem to think separation means withdrawal or erecting protective fences well back from this or that danger. But a close look at Daniel's life suggests that he saw separation not as a matter of dodging the hazard but of uniting the heart. His life reflects the spirit of David's prayer in Ps. 86:11, "Give me an undivided heart." And it foreshadows confidence in a promise God, through Ezekiel, made to the re-gathered exiles: "I will give them an undivided heart" (Ezek. 11:19).

Drawing on Daniel's Experience.

Roughly 2600 years separate Daniel's workplace from yours. And yet his story appears in the Bible to strengthen your faith in and walk with God. What lessons can you, as a Christian in the modern workplace—with all its godless practices—learn from these experiences of Daniel? I'll suggest four.

- *Know the spiritual risks in your work world.* From what God had revealed, Daniel knew the things in his work world that could "defile" him. You, too—from Scripture—should know which things in your workplace threaten your soul's health. Don't underestimate the power of the work world to confuse your priorities and blind you to God's purpose. Just as the earth's force of gravity constantly pulls objects downward, the world's display of lures constantly pulls at our flesh. The world parades many of those lures in the workplace. Organizational hierarchies create ladders to climb—appealing to selfish ambition. Salary scales promise higher pay, stirring up greed. The language of co-workers, the way they dress, the pressure to cheat or lie to beat the competition—all these forces and many others entice our flesh. Those who recommend that Christians stay out of the morally stained work world correctly understand one thing: the world does pose dangers to your spiritual life. Their error lies in their response to those dangers—a fear-driven retreat.
- *Decide to resist the rot, not to run from it.* The Bible includes not even a hint that Daniel pines to get back to the Holy Land and its kosher food. Instead, he settles down to work in the place God has put him and to face its challenges. By contrast, listen to the words of this quality control manager in a modern workplace: "I am spending a lot of time learning information and developing skills that are essentially irrelevant to the kingdom of God. I know that my teaching and

analytical skills could be used to promote God's kingdom directly rather than indirectly, and I long to apply myself to full-time service for Him." That's escapist thinking. It saps the spiritual strength and creativity needed to turn even the most secularized job into a platform for ministry. Jesus leaves no room for escapist thinking. In John 17:18, praying to his Father, he notes, "I have sent them into the world." That certainly includes the world of work.

- *Count on the sovereign God to work as you work.* Daniel's call through circumstances moved him from the Holy Land, where God had clearly been at work for centuries, to a land filled with phony gods. Yet even in Babylon, he found the sovereign God working in all things for his good—stirring favor with unbelievers. In his book, *S-t-r-e-t-c-h,* Gerard Kelly writes this about Daniel: ". . . in the deprivations of exile, he finds a new vision of the kingdom of God." In John 17:15 Jesus tells his Father, "My prayer is not that you take them out of the world but that you protect them from the evil one." Count on the sovereign God who has the power, even in your ungodly workplace, to protect you from the power of the evil one.

- *Strategize how to resist the rot in your workplace.* Daniel came up with a ten-day test diet. You'll need to develop strategies of your own to counter the unique temptations where you work. For example, if you're a man, the way a woman in your workplace dresses may create a potential stumbling block. Your strategy might be to train yourself to pray for the woman when tempted to look lustfully at her. Or if you're tempted with workaholism, your strategy might be to set self-imposed limits on your hours—perhaps giving some-one else permission to ask you hard questions as you make the adjustment. Ask God to lead you, by his Spirit, into those strategies that will both give him opportunity to work and also express your love for your co-workers.

The experience of a woman who works as a warranty submission specialist for an automobile dealer echoes these lessons from Daniel's wall of defense. Here, in her words, is her story: "In the course of my job, there are times when a less-than-desirable situation comes up that is very distasteful to me. It has to do with 'doctoring' a document so the company can profit from the job that was done. I am aware in my profession that it 'happens all the time' but the issue of truthfulness is very important to me. So important that when I applied for my current position, knowing that this type of practice goes on, I made it clear that I would not create or falsify information and I would not lie for my superiors.

"This has been interesting in several ways: I have never been asked to create or submit a document of this nature. If one comes across my desk, it is already finished and I just need to file it. If conversations pertaining to that type of situation begin in my office, it is moved to my superior's office and finished there. Finally when situations arise such as periodic audits that have to do with documenting the end result, I am likewise excused so that I do not need to defend something that I do not believe is right.

"My supervisor has been very astute in never placing me in a position to go against what I believe is right. From time to time I am able to have a conversation about the importance of being above board in everything we do and if I am ever asked to back up what I'm presenting, I am always prepared with a 'by the book' proof. If I am told that doesn't matter, I generally drop the conversation but create a document stored on my computer that briefly summarizes the dialog and lists specific details that would result. That helps me to cover my part to discourage the practice and keeps me from being part of the problem instead of part of the solution."

Like Daniel, this woman *recognized the situation as a spiritual risk in her work world.* She knew participating in falsehood would neither honor nor please God. She *decided to resist the rot, not run from it:* "I would not lie for my superiors," and yet she stayed on with the company. Although she does not say so explicitly in this account, she *counted on the sovereign God to work as she worked*. And finally, she *strategized how to resist the rot in her workplace*. Right from the time she began working for this employer, she made her standards clear. Then, as time passed, she helped develop procedures to carry out her strategy without alienating her boss.

Of course not all stories of the spiritual pollution confronting believers in the workplace end like this woman's story or Daniel's food test. Many contemporary Christians have suffered or even lost their jobs as a result of their refusal to comply with dishonest or immoral assignments. Sometimes this is the only possible outcome. Although Jesus warned us that the world will hate and persecute us, we need to take care to avoid a persecution complex. Some Christians seem to have the idea that every unbeliever automatically has it in for every believer. But Jesus himself was the friend of sinners. His main opposition came from religious phonies. So we should not go into the secular workplace with a chip on the shoulder—just spoiling for a fight with non-believers. Daniel's example shows us the value of looking for creative ways to stay true to our relationship with Jesus while preserving, if possible, the relationship with our co-workers.

A woman who works for a state agency had heard rumors that state workers were not allowed to display Bibles or anything religious that could offend someone. But, she says, "On my desk I keep a devotional, two different Bibles and a printed prayer. A 'sticky note' on my computer monitor says: 'God is in control.' These things have prompted people to ask me questions. So what I had heard about the limits on Christians in state employment turned out to be false."

But in some cases Christians overreact and bring avoidable persecution on themselves. For example, in 2002, a Christian man was one of more than 50,000 employees working for a well known employer in the United States. On October 11, known as

"Coming Out Day" among homosexuals, this man—along with a thousand other supervisors—received an email memo from his manager. The memo began: "If one of your employees elects to 'come out' at work, there are several things you can do to help that person feel comfortable in sharing his/her orientation in the workplace:" A list of bullet points followed, urging respect, support and sensitivity to employees who might "come out."

After reading the memo, the Christian man replied via his own email, sending his comeback to all 1,000 on the original mailing list. It read: "Please do not send this type of information to me anymore, as I find it disgusting and offensive. Thank you." He followed this with his name. When asked to apologize and promise never to do anything like that again, the Christian man refused. So the company fired him.

Was this the only option open to the Christian employee? Or could he have remained faithful with a different response and outcome? Before we explore this question, let's background it by recalling why Daniel landed in the lions' den (covered in more detail in Chapter Six). The issue then, with the anti-prayer law as with the defiling food, was *obedience*. Eating the king's food would have involved disobedience. Not praying to God and instead praying to a human king would have involved disobedience. In the food case, Daniel found a creative alternative. But in the prayer issue, he had to flat-out disobey the rules.

Back now to the Christian man who received the "Coming Out Day" email. Was the issue obedience verses disobedience? Understandably, the memo offended him. But what if he had simply chosen not to respond to it? This would have involved no disobedience to God. And what about his choice to distribute his reply so widely? Daniel, for example, involved only his two supervisors in the issue over not eating from the royal menu. And when it came to his illegal prayer, Daniel prayed in private. Although snoopers saw him praying, he did not turn it into a public display. What if the Christian who had been offended by the memo had taken the matter up with just the person who issued it instead of sending his reply to all 1,000 recipients?

Long before issuing the memo that had offended this man, the company had publicized its stance on diversity—even including much on the subject in its website. Perhaps this Christian's wisest strategy should have taken place earlier. Maybe he should have resigned and sought employment with another company whose policies did not clash with his convictions. Suppose you are convinced smoking is wrong and harmful. Why then continue working for and taking your paycheck from a company that makes its money selling cigarettes?

Each workplace issue that confronts you as a Christian will be unique. There is no pat answer or rule that will answer all your what-to-do questions. But by prayerfully relying on the Holy Spirit to guide you, you can do as Daniel did—look for creative strategies that will let you remain faithful to God while preserving a right and loving relationship with those in your workplace network.

Should Christians Follow Daniel's Example?

Daniel lived under the Old Covenant. Has God's will changed for us who live under the New Covenant? Should we—as many are urging—retreat from spiritually unclean workplaces to protect ourselves from contamination? In this area, what did Jesus do and teach? Isolation hardly describes his relationship with an unclean world. He lunched with people the religious crowd shunned. He actually made friends with sinners. He touched lepers, yet he himself did not become unclean. Instead, they became clean. And it's clear he expected his followers to enter spiritually hazardous environments as well, telling them, "I am sending you out like sheep among wolves" (Matt. 10:16). In prayer, Jesus specifically says he is not asking his Father to take his followers out of the world, but acknowledges that they will need spiritual protection in that world.

They, like Jesus himself, are sent into the world. As Christians, their assignment is the world.

Paul did not miss Jesus' clear example and teaching on our relationship with the world. In an earlier letter, Paul had instructed the Corinthian believers not to associate with so-called believers who continued to live immoral lives. The Corinthians misunderstood his point, thinking they should avoid immoral unbelievers. No, no, no, says Paul in I Cor. 5:9-11. I was "not at all meaning the people of this world who are immoral, or the greedy and swindlers, or idolators. In that case you would have to leave this world." Mingling with spiritually unclean people is part of our job description as Christians. Paul called the Philippian believers, ". . . children of God without fault in a crooked and depraved generation, in which you shine like stars in the universe as you hold out the word of life" (Phil. 2:15-16).

When the Israelites entered the Land of Promise, God prohibited their intermingling with people-groups who might infect them with any number of spiritual disorders. But now, under the New Covenant, God has lifted that ban. If we're no longer to rely on isolationism to keep us pure among pagans, what can we count on?

Your Spiritual Immune System.

God has given you an example—right in your own physical body—of his way of protecting you from the rot in your workplace. Just by living in this world, your body is surrounded by pollutants. Bacteria, viruses, microbes, toxins, parasites and so on pound away, trying to get inside where they can make you sick or kill you. What's your defense? Crawl into some plastic bubble and huddle inside its sterilized atmosphere? No. God has supplied you with an incredible immune system. If any of those enemy forces do enter your body, a whole army of defenders comes to your rescue. Your skin, thymus, white blood cells, leukocytes, lymph system—to name just a few of those defense forces—spring into action to preserve you.

In Christ, God has similarly provided you with a spiritual "immune system." That system includes an arsenal of weapons at your disposal as a believer.

- Because of the cross, you have been crucified to the world and the world to you (Gal. 6:14-15).
- So by the Spirit of Christ who lives in you, you can "put to death the misdeeds of the body" (Rom. 8:13).
- As the word of Christ lives richly in you, it makes you strong (I Jn. 2:14).
- The promises of God let you "participate in the divine nature and escape the corruption in the world caused by evil desires" (II Pet. 1:4).
- Jesus prayed that the Father himself will protect his followers from the evil one, right while they live in the unclean world (Jn. 17:15).
- God gave you your spiritual armor (Eph. 6:10-18) so you could resist rot such as you encounter in the work world—not run away from it.

Christian, your sovereign God is not limited to "pure" workplaces, to religious organizations or to so-called "Christian jobs." No—your God is the God of Daniel. Daniel found him to be just as powerful in Babylon as in the Holy Land. Your God is the God who loved everyone in the world so much he sent his Son to die for us. Your God is the God who raised that same Son from the dead. Trust him to work through you and your immune system, right there in your workplace, no matter how worldly it and your co-workers may appear to you.

Bottom line? Your spiritual immune system is the life of Christ in you. Your protection does not come from avoiding contact with the world (as if that were even possible!). Instead, as you trust Christ's divine nature—which includes holiness—to work in you, you find it acting as a filter even in the midst of unholy surroundings. A well worn joke has a young boy walking along a country road when he spots a bearded farmer hauling a wagonload of cow manure. "What are you going to do with *that* stuff?" the boy asks. "I'm taking it home to put on my strawberries," replied the farmer. "Weird," says the boy. "At our house, we put sugar and cream on strawberries." Even today, farmers and gardeners continue the practice. Some recent online advice for preparing the soil for a strawberry bed included these words: "To the soil I added a forty pound bag of cow manure. Rabbit manure is even better and easily transported from a local rabbit grower." What separates the delicious, perfectly pure strawberry from the smelly, decaying cow manure it was planted in? Just one thing—the life of the strawberry plant. Life triumphs over death. And the life of Christ in you will triumph over the corruption in your workplace.

An old song challenged Christians to "Dare to be a Daniel." According to Webster, to *dare* is "to confront boldly" and "to have the courage to contend against, venture, or try." God does not call us to be *daredevils,* reckless show-offs bent on self-serving adventure. Rather, he calls us to dare by being "strong and very courageous" (Josh. 1:7), like Joshua, to accomplish the others-serving mission on which he sends us. That mission is ministry, ministry right in the context of your daily work—the focus of Part Two.

PUTTING IT TO WORK

- What have you heard or read from other Christians who warn believers not to enter the world of work because of its hazards to spiritual health?
- Why do you think the God who warned his Old Covenant people not to intermingle with the ungodly nations now sends

his New Covenant believers into the sin-filled world of unbelievers?

- What are the spiritual risks in your work world?
- Describe any creative strategies you have used to stay right
  with God and still maintain relationships with unbelieving
  peers who press you to act in ungodly ways.
- To what degree might you have relied on isolationism to protect yourself against workplace impurity?
- How can you begin to trust God to work through your spiritual immune system as you confront difficult situations in your
  work?

SEEING WORK AS MINISTRY

Why do Christians find it so difficult to think of ministry in the workplace? To some, *workplace ministry* comes across as an oxymoron—like *freezer burn*, *liquid gas* or *only choice*. Could it be that the way we typically use the word *ministry* conditions us to think it doesn't mix well with the workplace? Consider these actual quotations from various sources:

- He left the ministry to seek secular work with more pay.
- . . . leaving their businesses or careers to enter the ministry.
- Eventually she left the ministry to return to college.
- Keith left the ministry to pursue business.
- [They] left the ministry for secular pursuits.
- Others quit the ministry for secular jobs.
- Everett soon abandoned the ministry for a teaching position.

The split-up between ministry and the workplace happened so long ago that today our Christian lingo simply takes it for granted they don't belong together. So it is extremely difficult for those in so-called "secular" work to conceive of what ministry might even look like in the context of a regular job.

Adding to the difficulty, we have come to associate ministry with what happens in the context of the institutional church—worship services, pastoral counseling, Bible studies, church programs and the like. Most real ministry gets done by authorized ministers, those with proper ecclesiastical titles or degrees. Trying to imagine how to transplant their church-oriented activities into the workplace boggles the mind.

To reunite *ministry* and *workplace* requires a return to the biblical definition of ministry. At root, the Greek New Testament words for it (*diakonos, diakonia* and *diakoneo*) speak of serving, helping, working. The NIV translates those words with some form of the word *serve* 43 times and some form of the word *minister* 19 times. In Eph. 4:12, Paul says "works of service [diakonos]" belong to all God's people, not just credentialed leaders. Most of God's people don't work in church-related jobs. So they must carry out their "works of service," their "ministries," in the roles they fill day in and day out. For many, that means a *workplace ministry* in a non-religious company or agency.

Part Two aims to help those in these workplaces visualize what *ministry* will look like there. Chapter Five explains that workplace ministry includes the work itself as it carries out God's command at creation to rule and subdue his earth for him. Chapter Six argues that as Christian workers do their work with integrity, they mirror God and the way he works (thus offering service/ministry to him). Chapter Seven emphasizes the call to serve (minister to) other believers on the job—Christian co-workers, bosses, subordinates, clients, customers and so on. And Chapter Eight defines another important part of ministry/service—the love for unbelieving workplace neighbors demonstrated in action and in word.

Because Daniel engaged in all these kinds of ministry, we can look to him as a model and a mentor.

CHAPTER FIVE

RULING: TENDING GOD'S EARTH

"Many Christians struggle with seeing the significance of the work they are called to do. They . . . often do not see the significance of the work itself."
  Joel Gillespie, "The Creation Mandate"

"And let the loveliness of our Lord, our God, rest on us, confirming the work that we do. Oh, yes. Affirm the work that we do."
  Ps. 90:17, The Message

Framing the Issue: Both the world-system and traditions of Christendom have devalued the work that occupies countless people. The world belittles low-wage jobs or those that offer no power or recognition. Christians, in exalting so-called "sacred" occupations, have seen little or no worth in "secular" work. Yet in the beginning, the working God created working human beings in his own likeness and delegated the care of his earth to us. We exercise that care through all kinds of work. Daniel's worldview included a biblical workview—which still serves as an excellent model.

Consider the apple. You pull a Honeycrisp from your lunch bag and bite into its crunchy, tart sweetness. Simple, isn't it? Or is it? A tale lies behind your seemingly effortless snack. And that story offers a micro-illustration of how God uses *people in ordinary workplaces* to sustain life on earth.

The Honeycrisp apple traces its ancestry to an Agricultural Experiment Station in Minnesota's Twin Cities. *Researchers* there crossbred the Keepsake apple with another variety, officially releasing the offspring, Honeycrisp, in 1991. From that beginning, the apple in your lunch bag may have arrived there via any number of routes. Let's imagine it happened this way.

An *entrepreneurial couple* in Wisconsin invests in land for a tree nursery. Seeing the market potential for such a long-lasting, taste-tempting apple, they gear up to propagate Honeycrisp trees for sale. They employ *nursery workers* who plant, fertilize, water and nurture the shoots to marketable size. Meanwhile, an *ad writer* in the nursery office prepares a catalog and website promoting the infant Honeycrisp trees.

In the Methow Valley of Eastern Washington, a *farm family* purchases 85 acres, with plans to turn it into an orchard. After reading the website on Honeycrisp, they order 1,000 plants. Then with a large tractor and *trained crew*, they plant their little "apple factories." From their county *extension agent*, they learn how to fight bugs, diseases and weather.

Four or five years later they begin to reap the fruit of their investment and hard work. The apple that will eventually reach your lunch bag hangs on a tree in the north part of the orchard. A *migrant farm worker* pulls your apple off the branch and drops it in a box. From there, a *trucker* hauls your apple to a warehouse, where *technicians* carefully control the temperature. Another *truck driver* transports your apple to a grocery store—the investment of another *entrepreneur*. A *stocker* puts your apple on display in the produce department. After selecting the apple, you take it to the counter, where a *checkout clerk* rings it up and bags it with your other groceries.

And after all those people put all that work into your apple, you're still able to buy it for less than you'd pay for a latte (behind which lies another story). Through the everyday work of those people, and more too numerous to mention here, God has sustained you with fresh fruit for your lunch.

Now think of all the workers in everyday jobs who make it possible for you to wear shoes. To drive a car. To invest your money. To learn accounting. To stay warm through a February ice storm. To drink pure water. To read a newspaper. To set a broken bone. It takes those and countless other kinds of work to make life on earth doable. But is work like that *ministry*?

When you hear the words "workplace ministry," what comes to mind? Activities such as witnessing to and praying for unbelievers, perhaps even some counseling? In a website article, Joel Gillespie points out that, "Many Christians struggle with seeing the significance of the work they are called to do. They see their work as a place for witnessing, for character building, for making money to support missionaries and church programs. But they often do not see the significance of the work itself. This is tragic. Anything about your job or your work which contributes to the good of other creatures, which helps care for and sustain them and make their life better, is a participation with God in His ministry of sustaining, preserving, and caring for His world."

In my experience, few of us see our *work itself*—the stuff spelled out in our job description—as part of our ministry. We're eager to serve God, but we don't think he counts planting an orchard, driving a truck or ringing up an apple as service. So we try to cram what we see as "ministry" into off-hours and weekends. Convinced that our work prevents us from engaging in "full-time ministry," we lead divided lives, split between a lot of meaningless work and a little ministry work. God's agenda, it seems to us, has shifted away from creation and now focuses entirely on salvation. Mentored by Daniel's biblically complete workview, we can begin to offer all parts of our unified lives as worship to God.

Daniel's Workview.

If we could ask Daniel whether he saw any ministry value in his daily work, he would probably answer with his own question: Why even raise the issue? Of *course* his job had ministry value. Daniel knew his Hebrew Bible. What from that Bible formed the foundation for his workview?

He knew that God, as "sovereign over the kingdoms of men," cares intensely for the earth he created and still sustains. Yes, the devil has inflated his own world-system, super-sized it to block our view and made it look as if God has abandoned the planet. But the fact still remains: "The earth is the Lord's, and everything in it" (Ps. 24:1). God's sovereignty, his absolute authority over his creation, formed the bedrock of Daniel's workview.

On that foundation rested the human element in his workview. The sovereign God delegated to human beings made in his likeness the authority to represent him by ruling the earth for him. At the very outset God declared that his human creatures would "rule . . . over all the earth" (Gen. 1:26). So Daniel understood the relationship between the earth God created and the human beings to whom he assigned its care and keeping.

Two verses later, God tells these human earth-rulers to "fill the earth and subdue it." *Today's English Version* captures the intent: "Have many children, so that your descendants will live all over the earth and bring it under their control." God was concerned with the whole earth—so it had to be full of the people he had created to manage it for him. The earth, God knew, was an unruly thing. He had put the raw materials all in place. But for creation to fulfill his goals, it would have to be ruled, controlled, brought into subjection. Weeds would try to choke out food-producing plants. Rain would pack soil, requiring cultivation. Animal populations might multiply and upset the balance. Terrain would impede travel and call for roads and bridges. The movement of tectonic plates below earth's surface would require earthquake-proof structures.

Some telling words in Genesis 2 illustrate this creation partnership between God, the Earth-Creator, and man, the earth-caretaker. Before God created human beings, "no shrub of the field had yet appeared on the earth and no plant of the field had yet sprung up, for the Lord God had not sent rain on the earth and there was no man to work the ground" (Gen. 2:5). The freshly created world contained the potential for these plants—perhaps in the form of seeds—but God delayed the irrigation and thus the growth until the human earth-tenders could report to work.

Daniel certainly knew all these passages. He had also read the prophet Jeremiah. On three different occasions in that prophet's writings God had called Nebuchadnezzar "my servant." How could God call this pagan his servant? Because, in spite of his spiritual blindness, Nebuchadnezzar was used of God in ruling over the earth—even in disciplining the proud and straying Israelites. The book of Daniel includes references to King Cyrus. Through Isaiah, God said of Cyrus, "He is my shepherd and will accomplish all that I please." (Is. 44:28). In a further word personally addressed to Cyrus, God said, "I will strengthen you, though you have not acknowledged me" (Is. 45:5). Both of these rulers—even though unbelievers—served the purposes of God. God saw them as his servants and shepherds. Daniel served under them. So in his everyday government job, Daniel served the servants of God. His work supported these "shepherds" of God, helping them carry out God's agenda in the world. Serving equals ministry.

If there had been any doubt in Daniel's mind that his everyday work was ministry, it surely would have been eliminated by his interpretation of Nebuchadnezzar's tree dream (summarized in Chapter Three). The dream itself came from God. The interpretation revealed God's continuing concern for the welfare of his earth and its creatures. The tree represented the rule of Nebuchadnezzar. The Nebuchadnezzar-tree (the king's responsibility for the Babylonian section of God's global orchard) provided safe shelter as well as "food for all" so that "from it every creature was fed" (4:12). In other words, Nebuchadnezzar's government kept anarchy and chaos at bay so that people and animals could lead peaceful and quiet lives. (Notice in I Tim. 2:1-4 how God wants kings to rule in ways that promote peaceful and quiet lives, producing conditions under which God's saving message can flourish.) We might picture Daniel's work as one branch of the Nebuchadnezzar-tree. In serving Nebuchadnezzar, the servant of God, Daniel helped to maintain the "tree" that God had planted to protect and sustain this territory on his earth.

The Bible does not tell us exactly what Daniel did in his various government roles throughout his career. In the beginning, he must have worked as what we might call an *apprentice*. English Bibles translate his later title in the Babylonian hierarchy with words such as *administrator* and *president*. After the Persians conquered the kingdom, Darius made Daniel one of three administrators over 120 "satraps" (governors of provinces). In Persian, satrap meant "protector of the province." At that level, Daniel probably spent his days focusing on a variety of oversight responsibilities. Writing rules to be followed by the satraps throughout the empire. Inspecting records. Making onsite visits to provinces to enforce compliance. Allocating funds (budgeting). Setting tax rates and establishing collection procedures. Ensuring proper law enforcement in cities and along roads. In other words, he probably dealt with many of the things that give today's top administrators headaches.

In Daniel's decades-long career in Babylon, he spent most of his days and hours and weeks doing *this* kind of work. Yes, he also spoke for God when he interpreted dreams and testified about God's coming kingdom and its King. But Daniel devoted the bulk of his time to serving God by carrying out the earthly king's business.

Building a Biblical Workview.

Patrick Klingaman says, "Work itself has no ministry value according to the Christians I've talked to." Think of the loss to the kingdom of God. Countless Christians spend most of their best hours in regular, non-religious jobs. As we've seen in Daniel, such work does have ministry value. But if you see your work as meaningless, trivial—even self-serving—and irrelevant to God's agenda, you'll find it impossible to do it wholeheartedly to the Lord.

Kevin Williams, an attorney, writes: "I have been trying for years to figure out my purpose for God on this earth. I feel like my life is caught in the mundane. . . . However, every time I try to break out of the mold that the world has placed me in, I find myself hopelessly trapped. . . .Until recently, I thought that secular work was beneath the 'spiritual' work of pastors and missionaries." Seeing his work in that light led Kevin to "feel the incredible burden of joyless work being placed back on my shoulders."

Unlike Kevin, Daniel lived and died centuries before Plato's influence taught later generations to divide the ideal from the material. So the sacred-secular dualism that still infects our thinking today did not weaken Daniel. He felt no tension between his everyday job and his work for God. For him, it was not either-or but both-and. Not secular work versus sacred work, but all of his work sacred, because he did all of it as service to God.

How, then, can you build a biblical workview? Begin with the foundation that supported Daniel's workview—the sovereignty of God over the earth that all belongs to and concerns him. This divine attention to the earth and its living beings calls to mind what God said to Jonah about the 120,000 people in Nineveh as well as their cattle: "Should I not be concerned about that great city" (Jon. 4:11). The God who created the earth and still holds it all together cares for it more than we can imagine.

Next remember that God has not set aside his first work assignment, to rule and subdue the earth, so that his will is done here on earth as it is in heaven. We might think that the God who spoke everything into being could simply have continued speaking to maintain this planet he cherishes. And maybe he could have. But for reasons known completely only to him, he chose to form human beings in his own image and to place us over the earth as his sub-rulers. How would we rule? Through our work. And planet-wide, the work would require an immense and diverse labor force.

An analogy may help. Sustaining human life on board the International Space Station (ISS) takes some doing. NASA calls the challenge of building and maintaining the space base "a very complex task." Spacecraft missions must continually replenish the supply of food and water for the ISS crew—a payload of more than 17,000 pounds in one recent visit. Even the repair of a space toilet required expertise and effort.

Keeping life livable on planet earth—God's "space station"—also requires immense and constant maintenance. God himself put the raw materials on board: soil, water, air, animal life, vegetation and so on. But he assigned to mankind a large role in maintaining this orbiting station. We might describe our role as *earthtending*.

Earthtending includes all the labor needed to keep this present world habitable as we await God's new creation. God is working out his purposes in his earth as it now exists. For example, he is providing a grace period in which people may turn from their sin to his Son. He is purifying his church. Preparing a body and bride for his Son. Building a temple of living stones. Forming an eternal family. And while God is carrying out these and other purposes, life here on space station earth must be sustained and maintained. Yes, the planet is currently in temporary bondage to frustration. The world-systems have fallen under the sway of the evil one. But this real property still rightly belongs to the One who created it. "He did not create it to be empty, but formed it to be inhabited" (Is. 45:18). He wasn't kidding when he said, "fill the earth."

Space station earth now orbits with more than 6 billion people on board. Maintaining an environment fit for human life is, in

NASA terms, "a very complex task." The task breaks down into what seems like an endless variety of earthtending. Earthtending—like the human population—has expanded immensely. Your job may not even have existed 50 years ago. Earthtending includes both paid and unpaid work. In 2006, the civilian labor force in the United States included roughly 150 million paid jobs. The amount and value of unpaid work cannot be calculated. Whatever niche your legitimate earthtending fills, you can do it as a service lovingly offered to God to help him maintain his earth and sustain life on this temporary planet. Your work itself has value both to God and to earth's inhabitants.

Just a few years after Daniel landed in Babylon, a letter arrived from the homeland. Jeremiah, the prophet, had sent it to the exiles and their leaders. It seems likely Daniel had read or heard the contents of this letter, because he says in Dan. 9:2 that he knew the writings of Jeremiah. Jeremiah wrote the letter to counteract the misleading influence of some false prophets among the exiles. They were urging the people not to put down roots, because they'd be going back home in just a short time. Not so, said Jeremiah's letter. Instead, on God's timetable, their exile would last 70 years. Babies born after their parents reached Babylon would be senior citizens by the time this whole expatriate experience ended.

So the counsel not to unpack their bags had it all wrong. The Lord was saying just the opposite: "Build houses and settle down; plant gardens and eat what they produce. Marry and have sons and daughters; find wives for your sons and give your daughters in marriage, so that they too may have sons and daughters. Increase in number there; do not decrease. Also, seek the peace and prosperity of the city to which I have carried you into exile. Pray to the Lord for it, because if it prospers, you too will prosper" (Jer. 29:5-7).

In a moment, we'll sift through those verses to visualize some of the occupations they imply. But first, stop to think about the how the situation of those exiles parallels that of Christians in the work world today. Just as they found themselves hundreds of miles from their homeland, our workplaces lie far from the visible kingdom of God. They were aliens, living among people who thought, spoke and acted in ways contrary to the revealed will of God. In the world's eyes, we're also weirdos. They were scattered. One here, a few there, but not gathered into a safe place protected by walls. During the workweek, we're also scattered. We may gather for an hour or two on Sunday and maybe again briefly midweek. But most of the time we're dispersed among unbelievers who, when they hear what we stand for, range from indifferent to downright hostile.

What kinds of occupations would naturally flow from the "settling down" God told these scattered people to do? *Build houses.* That means construction workers of various kinds. Suppliers of building materials. Transportation for those materials. Those skilled at repair. *Plant gardens.* Agricultural workers to plant, cultivate, and harvest. Cooks. Toolmakers to create shovels and hoes and cooking utensils. *Marry and raise families who do the same.* Stable family units need some sort of legal system to record legitimate marriages and births. Midwives. Educators. Perhaps librarians. *Increase—do not decrease.* Health care workers. *Seek the peace and prosperity of your Babylonian city.* Law enforcement and police protection. An economic system with bankers and accountants and investors.

While God wanted these exiles to settle down where they now lived, he would not directly supply what they would need to do so. Instead, most of what they needed would come indirectly through the work of people in various occupations. God wants his earth to be "filled" with human beings. To sustain us all, he has provided workers who will partner with him in supplying the many-sided needs of earth's population. In fact, Daniel—in his work of serving under Nebuchadnezzar—was actually carrying out God's instructions through Jeremiah to seek the welfare of the Babylonian community.

What God told these exiles to do would lead to two basic kinds of work: *providing* and *protecting*. The reign (rule) of Nebuchadnezzar, as seen in Daniel's interpretation of the tree dream, supplied the same two things—provision and protection. Through his own work, Daniel was helping to carry out God's original assignment for mankind, to "rule . . . over all the earth" (Gen. 1:26). As an assistant to the ruler Nebuchadnezzar, Daniel served God by earthtending, and his work both provided and protected.

Seeing Your Own Work as Ministry.

As you continue to build your workview, think of your own work. How does it help to carry out God's call to rule over the earth? In what way does it provide? In what way does it protect? I've found that very few Christians have thought through how their daily work fits into God's big-picture agenda. This may be new territory for you, so let's take a few examples just for practice.

This chapter began with the story of how a Honeycrisp apple might have traveled from its cross-bred beginning to your lunch bag. Let's choose any of the workers along that apple's path— say the ad-writer who wrote the copy in the catalog and website to advertise the tree starts for the nursery. He or she may have seen the job as simply a way of making money to pay the bills. But the questions, "In what way does it provide? In what way does it protect?" bring ad-writing into a much larger context. Writing apple-tree ads for a nursery fits into a long and interconnected series of jobs that provide nourishment for adults and children on God's earth. Seen in that light, the job becomes ministry (service).

Take another example. Imagine you're the construction supervisor on the school building in China that made international news (see Chapter Six). Knowing the forces this unruly earth can unleash, knowing the vulnerability of small children, how can you do your part in ruling and subduing the earth? In what way does your work provide? In what way does your work protect?

Think through the provide-protect questions for these occupational examples. (The job may call for one or the other. Perhaps both.)

- A retail clerk.
- A hospital janitor.
- A bus driver.
- A homemaker.
- A loan officer.
- A marine.
- A highway engineer.
- A nurse.
- An attorney.
- A cook.

Now answer the same questions for your own work. In what way does it provide or protect? As you ponder the answer, these additional questions may help:

How does God use your work to support you and your family? God honors the motivation to earn an income to supply the needs of your family. That's not a selfish goal. As Paul explained to Titus: "Our people must learn to devote themselves to doing what is good, in order that they may provide for daily necessities and not live unproductive lives" (Titus 3:14).

How does your work benefit those outside your family, regardless of their faith or lack of it, by supplying products or services they need? Think wide-angle. Your particular job may not result in the direct delivery of a product or service to individuals. But how does it fit into the mosaic of work done by other workers so that the combined labor results in provision or protection?

How does your work supply something needed by people-serving organizations? Think of your own church fellowship. How well would its meeting-place function if the world had no plumbers? Electricians? Refrigerator manufacturers? Road and highway engineers? Garbage collectors? Bankers? Police officers? Printers? Sound equipment manufacturers?

How might your work contribute to the upkeep of the earth itself? It's possible to take just about anything to the extreme—including environmentalism. But because the sovereign God made and cares intensely about his earth, we Christians ought to be concerned about how our work helps or hurts the air, water and soil of the planet.

How does your work make it possible for others to extend the gospel? Years ago, our family spent three weeks with a missionary aviation family in the jungles of Brazil. Before the airplane came, missionaries would spend days or weeks on a river to travel the distance a flight could cover in an hour. Think of the various kinds of work involved in the production of an aircraft. If you are a software engineer, how might your work—in the hands of missionaries—help to spread the good news?

How does your work help create or maintain peaceful and quiet conditions on earth? If you're part of the police force or the military, the question almost answers itself. Paul says we should pray for government leaders, "that we may live peaceful and quiet lives in all godliness and holiness. This is good, and pleases God our Savior, who wants all men to be saved and to come to a knowledge of the truth" (I Tim 2:2-4). It seems everyone wants peace and quiet. God wants those conditions, too. And he has placed many of his human workers in society to pursue those goals. *The Message* paraphrases Romans 13:4 in these "arresting" words: "The police aren't there just to be admired in their uniforms. God has an interest in keeping order, and he uses them to do it."

Kevin Williams, the attorney quoted earlier in this chapter, included this prayer in his blog: "Dear God, I beg You to change my heart about work. Take my joylessness away, and show me the awesome opportunity that I have right now to glorify You in the mundane." May God answer that prayer for you as Daniel's workview helps you build a new respect for your work as a God-given instrument for carrying out his agenda in the world.

Tending the earth, while one of the central activities in workplace ministry, forms just one part of it. In the next chapter, we'll see that Daniel's ministry included not only *what* he did but *how* he did it. Rather than doing work so typical of those shaped by this world's system, he reflected the excellence and workmanship of God.

PUTTING IT TO WORK

- In Patrick Klingaman's experience (see the quotation in this chapter), most Christians see no ministry value in their work itself. In your view, how do Christians typically evaluate the spiritual worth of their daily work?
- Why was Daniel able to see the value of his everyday work in Babylon?
- Historically, what makes it difficult for Christians today to see the value of the work itself?
- Reflect on what God told the exiled Jews of Daniel's day to do in their temporary quarters. What parallels do you see between their situation and yours?
- Six italicized questions appear near the end of this chapter. As you answered those questions, what new insights about your work came to mind?

CHAPTER SIX

INTEGRITY: WORKING TO MIRROR GOD

"Today's corporate world is lost in work's ethical wilderness"
  Norman L. Geisler and Randy Douglass, Integrity at Work

". . . our greatest need in the workplace right now is for Christians whose lifestyle and workstyle are so unique and so distinctive that coworkers will want to know why."
  Doug Sherman and William Hendricks,
  Your Work Matters to God

Framing the Issue: After creating heavens, earth, plants, animals and people, God pronounced it all to be very good. He always does excellent work. The heavens are constantly saying so (Ps. 19:1-3). But people easily ignore the message of creation. It's harder to ignore those who work right alongside us. And when those made in God's image do good work, co-workers see a reflection of the Creator and his work. Even Daniel's enemies could find no fault in Daniel's work. His walk backed up his talk.

The investors ranged from individuals to corporate giants, from a retired couple in Florida to the Royal Bank of Scotland. All of them had entrusted large sums of money to a man named Bernie Madoff. He had promised them returns as high as 46 percent. Fortis Bank lost $1.4 billion. An artist and author lost most of her life savings. All told the fraud totaled around $65 billion. Sentenced to 150 years in prison, Madoff is now living in the Federal Correctional Complex in Butner, North Carolina. "I have left a legacy of shame," he said. A prime example of *corrupt work*.

John Grisham's non-fiction book, *The Innocent Man*, tells the story of Ron Williamson from Ada, Oklahoma. Williamson, convicted of rape and murder, spent 12 years on death row and barely avoided execution. But—as finally proved by DNA evidence—Williamson was innocent. In his book, Grisham spells out why Williamson spent all those years in prison: shoddy, downright dishonest dealing by the police and the legal system. In short, *corrupt work*.

In May 2008, National Public Radio (NPR) reported that hundreds of school children died when their middle school building collapsed during an earthquake in China. One of the villagers, Wang Ming, said that "the building was poorly constructed and that the person in charge of quality control for the construction took bribes." Later, NPR reported that, "The parents believe there was too little steel in the building's structure, that its foundations weren't sunk deep enough and that there were no emergency exits." In short, *corrupt work*.

Corrupt work distorts. It no longer lines up with its original purpose or pure form. Corrupt work permeates our culture and cheats us out of benefits God intended us to enjoy. Now that Merriam-Webster has put its dictionary online, it monitors which words people look up most. In one recent year, the dictionary's most-searched-for word was "integrity." Does all this looking it up reflect a longing for more integrity? Or does all the looking it up

suggest many have forgotten what the word means? The dictionary defines integrity with terms such as *incorruptibility, soundness,
completeness* and *honesty.*

Daniel: Example of Integrity at Work.

A definition can nail the point, but an example hammers it home.
For a model of on-the-job integrity, consider Daniel. He got off to
a promising start as an administrator in the Babylonian government. He and his three Jewish friends faced the big boss, king
Nebuchadnezzar, in their first performance evaluation. With what
result? "In every matter of wisdom and understanding about which
the king questioned them, he found them ten times better than
all the magicians and enchanters in his whole kingdom" (1:20).
A-plus on Daniel's first report card.

But promising starters don't always finish well. Years pass.
More than 60 years elapse between Daniel 1 and 6. Years can
grind you down. Disappointments, two-faced co-workers, unfair
bosses, and temptations to cheat can blunt the cutting edge of
your principles. How is Daniel doing more than six decades after
his brilliant beginning? As chapter 6 begins, he is still promotable.
The new king, Darius, delegates authority to 120 governors. To
oversee them, he appoints three administrators—one of whom is
Daniel. Daniel performs so well the king plans to move him up
another notch. In Daniel's new role, even his former peers will
answer to him.

Peer Plan A: Find Fault with Daniel's Work. Word of
the upcoming promotion gets around. No way is Daniel going to
get this prize job if the other administrators and the governors can
help it. Eaten by envy, they dig for dirt on Daniel. According to
6:6, the administrators and the satraps act "as a group." That elite
crowd represents 122 leaders with political clout. They poke and
probe. Perhaps they interview those who've worked most closely
with Daniel. Possibly they dredge up old records from kingdom

archives. They "tried to find grounds for charges against Daniel in his conduct of government affairs" (6:4a). Had he taken a bribe in exchange for a favorable decision? Had he siphoned kingdom funds into his own pocket? Had he lied to cover up a scam? Try as they may, they find nothing to pin on Daniel. As Scripture puts it, "They could find no corruption in him, because he was trustworthy and neither corrupt nor negligent" (6:4b).

Peer Plan B: Attack Daniel's Faith. Unable to make a case against Daniel's work, they target his faith: "We will never find any basis for charges against this man Daniel unless it has something to do with the law of his God" (6:5). So they hatch a plan to manipulate the king into signing a temporary law. This law made it illegal to pray to anyone other than King Darius for the next 30 days. News of this law did not derail Daniel. His confidence in God stayed firm. He continued praying three times a day as usual, making no effort to hide the fact. Scripture says he thanked God (6:10) but says nothing about his asking protection from the hungry lions. In fact, it was King Darius who begged God to rescue his top administrator. As we know, God did rescue Daniel. Outcome: the king recognized and praised the true God. And although their meal came late, the lions breakfasted on satraps topped with administrators.

What Made Daniel's Work Such an Exception? Why did Daniel's enemies start with Plan A—the search for corruption in his work? Because ever since Adam and Eve, sin has corrupted not only human hearts but also human hands (work). As David puts it in Ps. 9:16, "the wicked are ensnared by the work of their hands." And Ps. 28:4 calls the work of the wicked "evil work." No wonder Daniel's enemies assumed they could find something smelly in Daniel's work. By ambushing Daniel and conning their king, they themselves were turning out corrupt work. So they naturally expected to find similar sleaziness in Daniel's performance.

Here's what they did not know: Daniel's right relationship with God had transformed his work. His enemies could find nothing wrong with his performance. This does not mean Daniel never sinned. But it does mean he did his work with such competence he gave his enemies no ammunition for sniping at it. Think of how even his enemies described his on-the-job performance (6:4). He was *trustworthy*. He was *not corrupt*. And he was *not negligent*. You could use those same words to describe God's work.

- God does trustworthy work. David recognized that God "is faithful in all he does" (Ps. 33:4). Ps. 111:7 says, "The works of his [God's] hands are faithful and just." "Great and marvelous are your deeds, Lord God Almighty. Just and true are your ways" (Rev. 15:3). As the God-Man, Jesus' work perfectly matched that of his Father. After hearing Jesus say, "You may go. Your son will live" (Jn. 4:50), a royal official took him at his word and headed for home. His servants met the worried father on the way with the news that his son's fever had broken at the same time Jesus had spoken.
- God's work is never corrupt. The products of human effort fail. Hard drives crash, roofs leak, companies go bankrupt. But "The world [the work of the Creator God] is firmly established; it cannot be moved" (Ps. 93:1). In Ps. 77:12-13 the psalmist says, "I will meditate on all your works and consider all your mighty deeds. Your ways, O God, are holy." When Jesus made wine at a wedding, insiders recognized the product of his work as "the best" (Jn. 2:10).
- God never does negligent work. Moses sang about God, saying "his works are perfect, and all his ways are just. A faithful God who does no wrong, upright and just is he" (Deut. 32:4). Isaiah exalted God and broke into praise because, "in perfect faithfulness you have done marvelous things, things planned long ago" (Is. 25:1). Jesus did not leave his work on earth half-finished. As he told his Father, "I have brought you glory on earth by completing the work you gave me to do" (Jn. 17:4).

Any co-worker looking at Daniel and his work saw a partial yet accurate reflection of the flawless work of the God who would later reveal himself fully in Christ. In a similar way, we who are being renewed in the image of our Creator are to reflect him in the way we do our work.

Without knowing the details, Daniel looked forward to what we look back on: the death and resurrection of Jesus. Because of Christ's death on the cross, God righted the wrongs that had separated us from him. As II Cor. 5:18 puts it, God "reconciled us to himself through Christ." But Christ's death did more than just reconcile God and sinful people. Through Christ God reconciled to himself "all things" (Col. 1:20). "All things" includes your work. In Christ, even your everyday work has been made right with God. You're no longer stuck with having to be content with the "corrupt work" so typical of this world. In his death and resurrection, Jesus has set you free from bad work. Instead, if you're a Christian believer, the wonderful good news is that you "are God's workmanship, created in Christ Jesus to do good works, which God prepared in advance for us to do." As a new creation in Christ, you are able to break away from the corrupt work pattern of the world. In Christ, you have the power to produce the good work that mirrors God's own work.

From Daniel's Work Life to Yours.

Your workplace is 2,500 years and perhaps thousands of air miles from Daniel's. The separation of time and distance is immense. Yet God can still use Daniel's experience in training you in the good work he created you to do. What insights can you take away from Daniel's work life?

Trust God, even when others oppose your faith. In spite of his excellent work habits, Daniel suffered workplace harassment for his faith. So may you. Like Daniel, make certain the opposition comes because of your faith and not because of faulty work habits. When the flak hit, Daniel kept trusting God. This gave God an opportunity to display his sovereignty even over the appetites of lions. If you become the target of workplace persecution for your faith, keep trusting eyes on Jesus and leave the outcomes to him. *The Message* paraphrases Jesus in these words: ". . . count yourselves blessed every time people put you down or throw you out or speak lies about you to discredit me. . . .And know that you are in good company. My prophets and witnesses have always gotten into this kind of trouble" (Matt. 5:11-12).

Expect co-workers to watch the way you work. Daniel's workmates were nitpicking him 2600 years ago. And the sin-warped human nature continues the finger-pointing today. Just watch how politicians dig up dirt to throw at each other. As a Christian in the workplace, you and your work may invite an extra amount of scrutiny from co-workers. Count on it: they *will* compare your talk with your walk. In Christ, your new self is "being renewed in knowledge in the image of its Creator" (Col. 3:10). So do your work in a way that mirrors that renewal and that image. Those three characteristics of Daniel's work serve as helpful reminders.

Do work everyone sees as right. Much as Daniel's rivals wanted to make Daniel wrong in the king's eyes, they had to recognize that his work was right. Although he lived more than 600 years before Paul wrote his letter to the Romans, Daniel practiced Rom. 12:17: ". . . do what is right in the eyes of everybody."

Although we human beings differ on countless questions, we agree on a surprising number of rights and wrongs. Just about everyone considers it wrong to misuse the Internet. In today's workplaces, sexual harassment ranks high on the list of wrongs. Give no one the slightest opportunity to charge you with inappropriate gender behavior. Guard the way you touch others, the jokes you tell, the pictures you display and the language you use. Examine your heart and words to make certain you treat clients and co-workers respectfully whatever their race, religion or sexual orientation. Even if you cannot agree with what they believe or do, they were made in the image of God and deserve your respect. Why? Because God himself is "kind to the ungrateful and wicked" (Lk. 6:35). And your work should reflect his.

Paul urged slaves (the employees of the first century) to show their employers "that they can be fully trusted, so that in every way they will make the teaching about God our Savior attractive" (Tit. 2:10). Through his work, Daniel demonstrated he could be fully trusted. And as a result, the king of the empire found the teaching about the saving, sovereign God attractive. Follow Daniel's lead as you work. Turn your work into activity that makes the Jesus way look good.

In sales jobs, the pressures to leave straight paths and take more profitable shortcuts can take the Christian into the red zone. One believer (we'll call him Bryan), who works as a regional sales director for a global pharmaceutical firm, recently felt the force of that temptation. His company had divided the U.S. market into 24 regions, rating, rewarding and recognizing each regional manager by how he or she compared with the other 23. After a new product came on the market, sales results in Bryan's region lagged results from most other regions. In spite of his best efforts, Bryan could not raise the sales for that product.

Frustrated and discouraged, he began asking other sales directors, "What are you doing to get such great results with this item?" They told him they had been promoting the product in ways not permitted by law. For example, they instructed their sales forces to market the drug for treating certain conditions, such as Lyme disease, even though no research data existed to back up their claims. Further, the FDA had not approved the drug for those diseases. Since Lyme disease was particularly prevalent in Bryan's region, his boss began leaning on him to take the pragmatic approach and adopt those sales techniques.

But Bryan saw this as a life-compromising path. "I can't do this," he said. "God calls us to honesty. This would deceive doctors and would lead them to deceive their patients."

"You're crazy not to do this," said many of his peers. But Bryan held his ground. It wasn't worth corrupting his own character, not to mention risking jail time. Instead, he met with his sales people to devise other ways to boost results for the new product. Sales increased somewhat, putting Bryan's region just slightly above average for all 24 districts.

Looking back, he's grateful for the way his decision affected two other regional managers—one from the northeastern and one from the southeastern U.S. These two saw Bryan's willingness to take a stand, met with him and agreed that they could not promote the product with dishonest spin. The three of them brainstormed to develop alternative marketing plans for their respective sales teams. In the end, all three kept their jobs. The other two thanked Bryan for setting an example and taking the lead in finding others who were willing to support each other in doing what was right. Although not Christian believers, these two—made in God's likeness—responded in a way reminiscent of Nebuchadnezzar to someone who reflected that likeness in his workplace decisions.

As he reflects on the experience, Bryan says, "In sales you're always compared with others who may do what you cannot do as a Christian."

Win trust by the way you work. While Scripture doesn't say it in so many words, it's a given that Daniel's co-workers knew they could count on him to produce quality work. If you make a commitment—not just by what you put in writing but by what you say—keep it. Follow through on promises to meet deadlines. If you're supposed to arrive for work at 8 a.m., show up on time. Don't consistently drag in at 8:15 or 8:20. If you handle money, do it with integrity, keeping records anyone can audit easily to verify your honesty. If you promise to send the report in on Friday, keep your word—or notify those involved if unexpected circumstances make it impossible. If you learn something negative about a customer or co-worker, don't feed it into the staff gossip machine—the peer shredder. If you make a mistake, own up to it and act to make things right. Never try to lie your way out of it. You trust God and his work. So he calls you to mirror his work by being trustworthy in yours.

If your supervisor assigns you a task, do it (unless complying involves disobeying a clear command of God). The so-called "household codes" of the New Testament show up in Eph. 5 and 6, Col. 3, Tit. 2 and I Pet. 2. All four of these letters include words to slaves. How, then, are slaves—even those working for pagans—to mirror God? The first instruction in all four of these household codes hits the same note: Eph. 6:5—"Obey." Col. 3:22—"Obey." Tit. 2:9—"Be subject to." And in I Pet. 2:18, slaves are to "submit" to their masters. So obedience, subjection and submission stand out when it came to the way slaves were to mirror God in their workplaces.

But today that "O" word and its synonyms offend many. According to one website: ". . . obedience must be just about the greatest of all evils. Obedience is surrender of personal power. Disobedience creates civilization. Obedience causes its collapse." In the world, obedience is for dogs, not people. Naturally, such an attitude breeds disrespect for those in positions of directing the work of others. "Obey" in those New Testament household codes translates a Greek word from which we get our word "acoustic." It means to listen attentively, then to act on the basis of having paid attention. If you only half hear your supervisor's instructions, how can you hope to carry them out?

How does working obediently image God? From Adam until now, what human being best mirrored the true God for us? Jesus Christ. And how did Jesus do that? By living as an obedient servant. The Bible says Jesus took "the very nature of a servant." He "humbled himself and became obedient to death—even death on a cross" (Phil. 2:7, 8). Another Scripture tells us Jesus "learned obedience from what he suffered" (Heb. 5:8). Christian, the spirit of Christ lives in you. To mirror God in your workplace, begin by bringing your words, attitudes and actions into line with his. Obey even when it hurts (as Jesus did).

Take responsibility—and follow through. In The *Message* paraphrase of Col. 3:25, Paul says, "The sullen servant who does shoddy work will be held responsible. Being Christian doesn't cover up bad work." In his book, *The 9 to 5 Window,* Os Hillman recalls: "Several years ago, I published a magazine devoted to Christians in the workplace. When I gave a copy to a friend, he looked at it and said, 'This doesn't even look like a Christian magazine.' What did he mean? He was saying the quality of many products that Christians produce tends to be less than the quality of non-Christian products—which is an indictment on the work of Christians." And a smudge on the mirror that supposedly reflects God's work.

Wasting time is another way of neglecting workplace responsibilities. A hospital employee told me the staff where she works has nicknamed one co-worker Waldo. When he, typically, fails to show up for work, they now ask: "Where's Waldo?" And the likely answer: out on the golf course. Salary.com surveyed more than 10,000 employees to learn how much time each was typically wasting on the job. The answer: 2.09 hours per eight-hour shift. That's more than 25 percent of the work time squandered. Judging by the survey, Salary.com estimated that on-the-job time wasting causes employers to lose $759 billion per year. Stealing time is stealing money. Not a reflection but a distortion of the way God works.

Yun, an attorney in Hawaii, says Christians need more help from the church in learning how to make right choices in the workplace. "In my job . . . I constantly need to make decisions with ethical implications. How do I make these decisions in a God-honoring way? Well, first I need to be aware of the ethical and theological dimensions of the situation. The role of the Church is to educate and train me to spot those issues. After teaching me to identify ethical/theological issues, the Church should provide theological guidance to help me resolve such issues. I cannot say that the modern church is structured in a way that enables its members to fulfill these two functions with great efficacy. It seems a rare occurrence that a church would devote a significant portion of its resources to grounding of members in the doctrine of vocation and its implications in everyday life. . . .

"If the church were to believe the doctrine of vocation with all its heart, it would structure its operations differently. It would not pay lip service to marketplace ministry by merely mentioning the phrase in a sermon. Even teaching on the subject is not enough. What's needed is the resourcing of church members to fulfill their vocations through counsel, active prayer coverage, encouragement—all kinds of spiritual arsenal the Holy Spirit has supplied the Church to fight the war against the enemy. The trick is to understand that the war is going on around us, and through vocations, God has strategically placed His beloved on every inch of the battlefield. It's time to launch a few grenades."

What if the church were to respond to Yun's plea for help? What kinds of issues might it address? For just one example, take Paul's word to slaves that they obey and submit to their masters. How does a 21st century employee translate those instructions into the modern workplace? Does the distinction between a slave then and an employee today make a difference in applying Paul's teaching? How can one obey and submit without acting as a "doormat" who wins only contempt and not respect? What fellow believers have faced workplace situations that illustrate responses in such cases?

Daniel and the "Chief End of Man."

The Westminster Catechism begins by asking: "What is the chief end of man?" The answer: "To glorify God and enjoy him forever." Judging by his career in Babylon, Daniel saw that as his main reason for working. The Genesis account of creation provides invaluable insight into what it means to glorify and enjoy God. Of all that he created, God made only us human beings in his "image" or "likeness" (Gen. 1:26, 27). How would we "image" or mirror God's likeness? God's next words provide an immediate clue: by filling, subduing and ruling over the earth and its creatures. In other words, by working. Our first glimpse of God in Genesis shows him working. God, the Worker, created in his image man, the worker. Why do we work? Because God works.

Genesis 2 confirms all this. Verse 2 says, "By the seventh day God had finished the work he had been doing; so on the seventh day he rested from all his work." Somewhere along the line, "the Lord God had planted a garden in the east, in Eden" (v. 8). And then, among the garden plants, God planted the man, to "work" the garden and "take care of it" (v. 15). The working God created the working human. We work because God does. And as we work in ways that make his ways visible, we both glorify and enjoy him. As Eric Liddell says in *Chariots of Fire*, "I believe God made me for a purpose, but he also made me fast. And when I run I feel His pleasure."

Here, then, lies your primary reason for working: to image God. Yes, *image* is a noun—but it's also a verb. Webster says the verb to *image* means *to reflect* or *to mirror*. The crew of a submerged submarine cannot see the aircraft carrier that floats on the surface. So they depend on the images they can see by means of the mirrors in a periscope. The images are not the carrier itself, but they faithfully represent the carrier so that the crew can identify and deal with it.

Like that carrier, God is invisible. He is especially hidden to those still submerged in sin. But as one whose eye of faith has seen God in the face of Jesus Christ, you play a "periscope" role in your workplace. By the way you work—which includes the way you think, speak and act—you are there to mirror the true God. By observing you in your work habits, your co-workers should be able to catch glimpses of what the real God is like. They may or may not eventually respond to God by trusting his Son. In either case, you serve God's purpose and please him simply by faithfully representing him and his work in the way you work. Up periscope!

Your co-workers who observe what you reflect probably include two kinds of people—those who are trusting and following Christ and those who are not. Chapter Seven will concentrate on your responsibility to the Christian brothers and sisters in your workplace. Again, Daniel will serve as mentor as we watch him in relationship with his fellow believers.

PUTTING IT TO WORK

- Describe two or three examples of corrupt work you have seen in or around your workplace. In each case, how did that kind of work distort a truthful conception of God?
- At root, what motivated Daniel's enemies to attempt to do their dirty work against him? (See Eccles. 4:4.) In what ways have you seen this motivation playing out in your workplace?
- Identify five opportunities your work provides to mirror the way God works.
- In what ways might your work be projecting a misleading picture of God? How can you change that?
- Honestly evaluate your relationship with your boss. Does your attitude point toward the obedient-servant attitude of Jesus?

CHAPTER SEVEN

COMMUNITY: FINDING AND SERVING FELLOW BELIEVERS

"The church in the workplace is the purest form of the body of Christ today due to its diversity."
    Os Hillman, International Coalition of Workplace Ministries

"How can we identify other Christians at work? How can we engage in relationships based on prayer and encouragement?. . . I feel totally lost in terms of taking that first step. . . ."
    From a blog headed, "How Do We Forge Real Community at Work?"

Framing the Issue: As a believer in your workplace, you may feel isolated, cut off from the support and encouragement of other Christians. At one point, Elijah thought he was the only one left still following God. Actually, he was simply unaware of several thousand others. As you face on-the-job pressures, you and other Christians there need more than a smile and nod on the weekend from believers you hardly know. If possible, you need to find and network with each other at work. Daniel did.

If you're up against the Boston Red Sox, you don't face them all by yourself. Instead, you meet the challenge as part of a . . . *team*. If you're breaking up hard ground with an old-fashioned plow, it's better to pull it not with just one horse but to hitch up a . . . *team*. If you're a surgeon doing bypass surgery on a patient with blocked arteries, you would do so only as one member of a surgical . . . *team*. Who thought up the idea of a team? The advantages of a team seem to be built into the way things are. After God made the heavens, earth, light, sky, oceans, land, plants, animals and man, he looked it all over and found everything to be "very good." But then, after putting Adam to work caring for the Garden of Eden, God found a flaw. In God's words, "It is not good for the man to be alone." So God created Eve, and the two became a . . . *team*.

God built the benefits of teamwork into his creation. Why? God made us in his likeness—and God himself lives and works as a team: Father, Son and Holy Spirit. They are perfectly united. And yet each of the three Persons in the one God contributes something unique to accomplishing God's purposes. Seamless teamwork!

The Teacher who wrote Ecclesiastes, observing creation, saw the advantages of teamwork. Here's how *The Message* paraphrases his words: "It's better to have a partner than to go it alone. Share the work, share the wealth. And if one falls down, the other helps, But if there's no one to help, tough! . . . By yourself you're unprotected. With a friend you can face the worst. Can you round up a third? A three-stranded rope isn't easily snapped" (Eccles. 4:9-12).

Daniel as Team Player.

In this chapter we take another look at Daniel in his workplace. We've seen him remaining strong in his faith and witness in a pagan work environment. How? By "seeing" the coming Kingdom of God and making it, rather than the kingdom of Babylon, his priority. By knowing who he was in spite of efforts to change his identity. And by keeping his heart detached from anything that would pollute his relationship with God. Those personal strengths might lead us to imagine Daniel as a loner. In fact, that old song says, "Dare to be a Daniel, *dare to stand alone*." But Daniel did not stand alone. He was no isolated individualist. Instead, he cultivated his relationship with other believing co-workers. Here lies another secret of Daniel's strong finish: he worked as part of a team. And in doing so, he set an example for working Christians to follow today.

Partnering under Peer Pressure. Any workplace will have its own forms of urging those who work there to conform to what the in-group thinks, says and does. Daniel's government gang was no exception. As we saw in an earlier chapter, some of the Babylonian ways presented no problem to a Jew who worshiped the true God. Apparently, for example, it was okay for them to be called by the pagan names the Babylonians assigned. But other practices conflicted with deeply held convictions. Daniel knew what God's Law said about separation. For example, "You must keep the Israelites separate from things that make them unclean" (Lev. 15:31). And for the young Jewish guys, the royal menu would "defile" them, or make them unclean (Dan. 1:8).

As we saw in the chapter on separation, "Daniel resolved not to defile himself with the royal food and wine." That could sound as if Daniel took up this minority position all on his own. But reading between the lines, we can see that Daniel and his three Jewish fellow-apprentices must have talked this issue over among themselves. Because when Daniel proposed the experimental diet (1:12), he said to the guard over all four of them, "Please test your servants . . ." [plural]. Daniel would hardly have committed the other three to such a test unless they had previously agreed to the plan.

Everybody else was eating from the king's menu. Imagine

being the odd-man out with only veggies and no choice cuts of meat on your plate. "Hey, Danny boy—real men eat pork!" The pressure to go along with the crowd must have been intense. But Daniel didn't have to handle this pressure alone. During the ten days of the test, at least three fellow believers among his co-workers were also eating meatless meals. The support of a team made the test more tolerable.

Collaborating through Crisis. Believers at work face not only peer pressure but crises of many kinds. Work—God's good gift from the beginning—became more difficult as a consequence of sin. The "thorns and thistles" of Gen. 3:18 graphically represent the endless sharp and painful emergencies that crop up in the workplace. For Daniel in chapter 2, top management—the king himself—created the crisis. A troubling dream (which, as we have seen, foretold God's coming kingdom) kept Nebuchadnezzar from sleeping. Not knowing what it meant, the king not only demanded that his metaphysical gurus interpret it but also that they tell him the details of the dream itself. If they could accurately narrate the dream without being told the plot line, then the king could trust their explanation of what it meant. The king's experts told him the obvious: what he asked was humanly impossible. So in a fit of impetuous rage, Nebuchadnezzar spat out the order to kill "all the wise men of Babylon" (2:12), including Daniel and his Jewish buddies. Workplace crises don't get much worse than this one!

When Daniel gets wind of the blanket order for execution, he does two things. First, he visits the head of the death squad and asks for and gets a delay so that he can do as the king has asked. Second, he meets with his believing co-workers and asks them urgently to pray for God to intervene and reveal the dream to him. They pray. And sometime that night, God reveals to Daniel both the dream and its interpretation. After thanking God, Daniel goes to the king and tells him accurately the details of the dream as well as its meaning. Amazingly, this pagan worshiper of false gods acknowledges that Daniel's God "is the God of gods" (2:47).

This ends the crisis—for Daniel, his three friends and the rest of Babylon's wise men. Although God reveals the mystery through one man, Daniel does not face this workplace crisis alone but as part of a team that prays.

Sharing in Success. The outcome of this crisis highlights a third example of the team spirit among Daniel and his believing co-workers. Not only did the grateful king recognize the true God as the superior of all others gods, he also promoted Daniel, making him "ruler over the entire province of Babylon" and the chief "over all its wise men" (2:48). So Daniel's career path rocketed him from trainee to top dog in a single step. But even with his sudden success, he did not think or act individualistically. As the text says, " . . . at Daniel's request the king appointed Shadrach, Meshach and Abednego administrators over the province of Babylon" (2:48). Success did not go to Daniel's head. He thought and worked as a team member even when the spotlight landed specifically on him. He did not hoard his success but shared it with his believing co-workers.

In his workplace partnership with other believers, Daniel pictures Jesus. Jesus, working always with his Father and the Holy Spirit, worked also with the team of 12 who surrounded him. Like Jesus and like Daniel, we need to see the value of linking hands with other believers in our working circles.

Our curiosity about Daniel's small group might raise more questions than the Bible answers. When did they meet? Did they gather regularly or just now and then? Did devoted Jews in addition to these four assemble with them? What made up their agenda when they met? What restrictions might their jobs or their supervisors have imposed on their ability to gather freely? While these and similar details might intrigue us, knowing them might tempt us to copy the outward forms of their get-togethers. Instead, the Daniel account gives us precisely what we need to know—that Daniel faced his workplace trials not with a lone-ranger, just-God-and-me attitude, but as part of a team.

Daniel and his friends model for us the believer-to-believer encouragement so valuable to the Christian whose calling places him or her in one of the world's workplaces. Does your work require you to relate to co-workers, supervisors, clients, suppliers or others? If so, which of them are believers? According to The Institute for the Study of American Evangelicals at Wheaton College, "One of the most difficult things to establish about evangelicals is a precise estimate of just how many of them there are in the United States." But in light of several surveys, the Institute says that "a general estimate of the nation's evangelical population could safely be said to average somewhere between 30-35% of the population, or about 100 million Americans." Christians not defining themselves as "evangelical" would swell this number. That means if you live in the United States, you're likely to have regular workplace contact with other Christians. Even so, it's possible that your work places you where you're the only believer. Joseph apparently found himself in that position after his brothers sold him into Egypt.

If your day-to-day work relationships include no other Christians, you may want to connect with believers who, although not on the same payroll, work in the same field. In his book, S-T-R-E-T-C-H, Gerard Kelly envisions a church that equips people for "works of service in the world . . . loving where others might hate, working with a passion because work is worship." Such a church, he says, would nurture "networks of friendship and mutual support [that] will connect believers to others in the same field and calling." He dreams of a church where there are "prayer meetings for dentists and think-tanks for nurses; where teachers meet to talk together of the kingdom possibilities in their schools; where people who have known success in business take time to mentor and equip the unemployed; where artists and photographers and DJs and web designers seek each other out to create vital sparks of prayer and interaction."

Forming Your Workplace Network.

Kelly makes it clear that such a church exists only as his "dream." Meanwhile, if your church fellowship does not foster such interaction, what can you do to link arms with other believers in your workplace or your field of work? How can you form a network of mutual support? And in the pressured, non-religious context of the workplace, what does mutual support look like?

The First Challenge: Recognition. In an office, shop or classroom, you'll need to identify some others believers before you can begin any kind of networking for mutual support. For Daniel, Shadrach, Meshach and Abednego, recognizing each other posed no problem. They probably knew each other before their abrupt, involuntary transfer. Even if they had never met, their accents must have tagged them as belonging to that group of foreigners from Judah. But for us today, recognizing other believers doesn't happen quite so easily. Life in an organized church can leave our Christian-detector skills undeveloped. Why? Because we've learned to depend on external "badges." I recently volunteered to mentor a student in a local elementary school during one lunch-hour each week. Before the first session the school issued me a badge with my photo on it. As I walk the hallways of the school, I can feel the eyes of teachers, administrators and even cafeteria staff studying me and then fastening on my badge. Once they see it, they smile and nod. I'm one of them. I belong.

In the typical church crowd, our badges may be less formal but they're just as real. The mere fact that someone shows up week after week in our church meetings tends to identify him or her as a fellow believer. Carrying a Bible has the badge effect. We listen to speech patterns. Do they speak Christian-eze, fluently using words like "blessing," "worship team," "spiritual gifts" and "saved"? Fish symbols on car bumpers, cross jewelry and WWJD bracelets also help. Of course non-Christians can display any or all of these markers, so such signs prove nothing. But after years of depending on them, our ability to recognize other believers can atrophy.

If you, like Elijah, feel like the "only one" (I Kgs. 19:10) where you work, begin your network-building with prayer. During a recent coffee time with a friend, he told me that he feared that the language and culture of his workplace had begun to take its toll in his speech and relationships with others. I asked him if he knew of any other believers among his co-workers. He did not. So I suggested that we begin to pray that the Lord would bring him into contact with one or more other believers. A few weeks later he announced that he had discovered another believer in his unit who had begun regularly meeting with two others—and that they had invited him to join them. The God whose Son promises to be with believers who gather in his name loves to answer prayers for such workplace networking.

While you pray, you can stay on the alert for answers. Spotting other believers in the workplace presses us back to Jesus' words, when he said, "Each tree is recognized by its own fruit" (Lk. 6:44). As you set out to look for fellow believers in your work circle, it may help to develop what I call "fruit questions." These are questions you can ask yourself as you observe and listen to co-workers, clients, customers, contractors or what have you. Think of questions in two dimensions, suggested by the vertical and horizontal lines of the cross.

Vertical fruit questions help you discern how others are relating to God. Examples:

- How do they treat the name of Jesus?
- If they see a Bible or hear it mentioned, how do they respond?
- Do they identify themselves as Christians—even when doing so may bring ridicule?
- What seems to be the basis of their hope?

Horizontal fruit questions to help observe relationships with fellow humans. Examples:

- How do they treat the "nobodies" among co-workers or clients?
- Do they forgive others who wrong them?
- When co-workers mess up, do they respond with patience or irritation?
- Do they respect supervisors—even when they're not around to hear?

Of course these questions and others like them—alone—will give you only clues, not bullet-proof evidence one way or the other. Keep in mind, too, that in examining fruit you are not trying to play God by pronouncing whether a person is eternally saved or lost. Instead, you're simply looking for signs that will lead you into mutually supportive relationships with other believers in your network who are also engaged in the struggle of faith. Don't expect your search to be easy. It will probably be messy, not fitting into any pre-conceived pattern.

Intentionally connecting with believers in any workplace can take you out of your comfort zone. Doing so in a military setting can present even greater challenges. Ryan, a friend of mine, tells me that some Christians in the military, intimidated by their surroundings, blend in as closet believers. The atmosphere oozes with worldly pride over issues like strength, speed, shooting skill and ability to handle stress. Pornography is blatant. Deployed twice in Iraq, Ryan says, "Most new Christians remain quiet about their faith."

Even after Ryan's recent return to the States, he continues to meet with and encourage some of the military men he served with overseas. I asked him: "What circumstances did God use in your discovery of other Christians in the army while in Iraq?" He told me that although he had positional authority, he tried to cultivate relational authority as well. He said, "It took time to make spiritual conversation possible. I had to win the right to be heard. In many cases, although certain guys said they were Christians, it had no effect on their behavior." He then told me the "messy" ways he came to discover four men who shared his faith in Christ.

The first noticed Ryan's displeasure when he saw another soldier behave unacceptably. "Why are you so upset?" the man asked him. Ryan replied, "Because I'm a Christian and it troubles me to see people act that way." The man looked puzzled. "Well, I'm a Christian, too, and things like that don't bother me." This exchange opened the way for further conversations about spiritual realities.

The discovery of a second Christian came about as a result of airing political views. The team's previous leader had been outspokenly liberal. After Ryan replaced him, one of the team members became boldly vocal about such issues as big-versus-small government, gun control, global warming and the school system. Then, Ryan said, the discussions went to issues like evolution, creation and abortion. When Ryan agreed with most of these views, the man said, "So then you must be a Christian, too."

Ryan noticed that a third man had a cross tattooed on the back of his hand. Ryan asked about it—and discovered a fellow believer. An external badge, to be sure, but one that led to a deeper look.

A fourth Christian surfaced while Ryan and he were working together in an armed forces booth displaying military equipment. The two of them sat atop a Humvee, working with a 50-caliber machine gun. An attractive woman strolled past the booth. "Hey, said Ryan's partner, "check that one out!" Ryan shook his head and said, "My God doesn't want me to do that." The other soldier bristled: "I have the same God as you do." Ryan went on to mention Jesus' words about lustful looking amounting to heart adultery. The man became silent. Then, about 15 minutes later, he asked, "Isn't it okay to at least notice that a girl is pretty?"

What followed paved the way for further conversation about the Christian life.

What might be called "brand loyalty" can hamper our ability to recognize other Christians in the workplace. In Gal. 6:10 Paul says, "Therefore, as we have opportunity, let us do good to all people, especially to those who belong to the family of believers [literally, 'household of faith']." Should we interpret the "household of faith" as referring to those believers who share my church brand, who belong to my denomination, who attend my local assembly? Or should we interpret "those who belong to the family of believers" more inclusively? Am I to extend my support to the wider circle of Christians at work?

The brand loyalty understanding makes life less complicated. I'm more comfortable relating to people who share my church traditions and interpretations. I understand them. They understand me. They're easier to spot. But the household of faith extends far beyond those who wear my label. Seeing the household of faith requires me to view life from a kingdom-of-God (rather than an institutional-church) perspective. If co-workers or clients are trusting Christ and his work on the cross as the basis of their relationship with God, I need to accept them because Christ has accepted them (Rom. 15:7). They may hold some doctrines or follow some practices I disagree with, but through kingdom-of-God lenses I see them as brothers and sisters in Christ.

The Second Challenge: Response. Once you've discovered other believers in your workplace network, what responsibility, if any, do you as a believer have toward them? As we saw in Chapter Two, kingdom ambassadors serve others who share the same citizenship. Reading Gal. 6:10 from that kingdom-of-God viewpoint stretches our understanding of "as we have opportunity." It adds a whole new dimension to the dozens of forms of "one-anothering" called for in the New Testament. A few examples:

• Encourage each other every day

- Care not only about your own welfare but also that of others
- Live harmoniously with each other
- Lay down your lives for each other
- Think about how to spur one another on in loving action and practical help
- Don't grumble about each other
- Show kindness and compassion to one another
- Forgive each other
- Don't insist on your own way but give in to each other

To take just the first example, how can believers "encourage one another daily" (Heb. 3:13) within the limited-contact context of the typical institutional church? Let's say my church directory lists 200 members. Typically I'll have little or no contact with most of them during the week. That translates into little or no opportunity. But through my work, I'll probably have frequent contact with other members of the household of faith—and therefore many opportunities to serve them in love. These opportunities come through what many are calling the church in the workplace.

Daryl Miller has worked in the environmental services department of a hospital for 22 years. But he did not originally intend to work in this role. Here is his story: "I was heading toward the ministry, so I completed regular Bible college and seminary training. But while I thought I was going to be a pastor, things did not work out that way. So I returned to what I had done to earn my way through school: janitorial work in this hospital. But I was not happy in this role. I tried hard to get into something else—anything else.

"Thinking I might become a chaplain, I enrolled in a clinical pastoral education training program in another hospital. During my second quarter there, I visited an older patient who had served as a pastor. As I spoke with him, I must have voiced some negativity about being a janitor and not in the ministry. He looked me straight in the eye and said, 'But you are in the ministry.' God used his words to change my whole attitude. Suddenly, I no longer looked at the hospital as just a place to work. Since that time, God has used me in many ways in people's lives—ways I could never have imagined.

"One man (I'll call him Mel), a fellow janitor, had been an alcoholic. He had divorced his Christian wife. But some time after that, he had opened his heart to Jesus. In time, he married a wonderful Christian woman who also works here at the hospital. He and I did a lot of talking and counseling. I urged him to memorize Scripture. 'No,' he said, 'I can't memorize. My education ended in grade school.' But I persisted, starting him with a few basic verses. He found out he could memorize God's Word. As he grew, I discovered he had a real gift in dealing with people. Mel's job later required him to handle infectious waste, which resulted in his contracting hepatitis. But his testimony, even as he recovered from a liver transplant, inspired everybody.

"'Joe,' another man who still works at the hospital, had twice been jailed for domestic disputes. He never felt loved by his mother and hardly knew his workaholic father. His brothers were too much older to pay much attention to him. So he didn't have a lot of social interaction with anyone. But through the years I've worked with him, teaching him Scripture and helping him understand how things work here in the hospital. I provided him (as I did Mel) with a good study Bible.

"Not long ago, while walking down the hallway, I met 'Judy,' an admitting clerk in the mother-baby unit. I knew her only slightly. When I asked how she was doing, she broke down. Then she poured out her story. Her son had died—most likely a suicide—just a few months earlier. I listened, prayed with her and did what I could to encourage and comfort her. I still check on her now and then to see how she's doing. I'm not sure whether she is a believer.

"In working with Judy and similar situations, I rely on other Christians in what I call the hospital 'prayer chain.' As I make my janitorial rounds, I'll say to one believer after another, 'Please pray for me. I'm not really qualified to help in this case. It's requiring more of me than I have to offer.' So whenever someone is helped, I know it's not me. Instead, it's God—using me and all these others who are praying.

"My work puts me into contact with many people, and that's where the momentum of this ministry lies. God has placed me where I can talk to others, learn their needs and ask, 'Would you like us to pray?' On any given day, I can usually get to 10 or 15 believers in the prayer chain. All told, I probably know of 30 to 40 believers in the various hospital departments.

"This ministry has blossomed in ways that have benefited my family. It's not unusual for me to return home and tell my wife and kids, 'Okay, we need to pray for this or that person.' They know some of the people on the prayer chain by name—often because they have walked around with me while I work. Had I chosen my own way, I would now be pastoring a church. But this, not that, was what God wanted me to do. Knowing that, I need to do my work well. I'm here to serve—and that's what 'ministry' means."

"Ministry" in the workplace will take different forms than we're accustomed to in church programs. You were hired to do your work and to do it at the right time—and you may offer your work itself to God as worship. Never steal your employer's time in the name of "ministry." Be creative. Use lunch hours. Rest breaks. Periods before and after work. Weekends. Socialize in your home or in restaurants or coffee shops.

Delegate ministry to others. One Christian said, "My position placed me where others could pop in anytime to share and/or pray together. On a recent afternoon, four men stopped by for that purpose (they all came separately for my individual attention), but I was too busy with customers. I introduced them to each other and they continued to share and encourage each other in their struggle and needs. Isn't God's family great?"

Daniel "went about the king's business" (Dan. 8:27). But he

also networked with other believers in his workplace. Within your context, learn how to follow his example. Believing co-workers, though, probably make up a minority of those you interact with in a typical work week. As you serve your brothers and sisters in Christ, be careful to avoid any favoritism that would lead you to treat unbelievers less than fairly. In Chapter Eight we'll observe how Daniel related to his unbelieving workplace neighbors.

PUTTING IT TO WORK

- Looking back, in what context have you felt the responsibility to serve other believers? In your church fellowship? In your workplace? Both? Illustrate your answer.
- In your opinion, what often prevents believers from identifying each other in workplace settings?
- List any others you believe are Christians within your job-related network (co-workers, supervisors, clients, vendors, etc.)?
- If you're not aware of any other believers in your work circles, what steps will you take to try to find some?
- In terms of your own workplace situation, what kinds of opportunities for mutual encouragement are possible to you and any other believers?

CHAPTER EIGHT

RESPECT: LOVING UNBELIEVERS

"... as we have opportunity, let us do good to all people. ..."
  Gal. 6:10

"You cannot turn respect for unbelievers into a technique. You know, I am going to respect unbelievers so that I might win them, just like I am going to give them a bowl of soup that I might win them."
  Jerram Barrs, Professor, Covenant Seminary

Framing the Issue: Too often, the longer we Christians associate with fellow believers, the fewer unbelievers we befriend. Sometimes we're just not comfortable with people who think, talk and act in ways God has delivered us from. But the New Testament encourages continuing interaction with unbelievers. Daniel did not sever his relationship with pagan workplace neighbors. His example still points us in the right direction.

You've been at your new job just a month, but already you've discovered:

- *The boss's wife—with his encouragement—just underwent an abortion.*
- *The unmarried woman who delivers inter-office mail is living with a man.*
- *You've been placed in the same work group with someone who is HIV positive.*
- *Your main customer, a female, has just married another woman.*
- *Your next-cubicle co-worker has lined his space with pictures that offend you.*
- *The computer network specialist assigned to your unit constantly uses the F-word.*

How do you—one of the few Christians in the office—respond to these people? How do you treat them? How do you secretly view them? Would you eat lunch with them? Invite them into your home? Do you judge them? Tolerate them? Try to avoid them?

It seems everybody needs somebody to look down on. In the fifth century, Egyptians looked down on Romans. Romans scorned the French, who in turn frowned on the English. Now many Europeans consider Americans barbarians. And you may know Americans who hold a bit of contempt for Canadians.

Even if you're not looking down on someone else, you may be fighting feelings of being looked down on. That can be the plight of Wal-Mart shoppers. Of stay-at-home-moms (or dads). Of working moms. In Timothy's day, some church people slighted him as a leader because he was young. Religion probably provides one of the loftiest perches from which one can peer condescendingly down on others. But religious contempt is just one rung on one of many ladders from which we humans can look down on co-workers in the world of work. Such high-mindedness leads to what we today call "workplace discrimination." Age, obesity, pregnancy, whistle-blowing, plus the old standbys of gender, race and religion, can each create scorners and scornees—and even bring the parties face to face in court.

The new verb, "to diss," recently joined the slang family. "Dissing the boss" has become a trendy way to describe words or actions that communicate contempt. In a working world of dissers, Daniel stands out as an exception. From the vantage point of self-centered human nature, he would have had both religious and political reasons to look down his nose at those above him in the Babylonian hierarchy. They were Gentiles—outsiders, pagans who neither knew nor worshiped the true God. They were enemies—conquerors who had ripped Daniel and his friends up by their roots and transplanted them in foreign soil.

As God's "chosen people," Jews who lived a few hundred years after Daniel would turn disdain for non-Jews into almost an art form. According to the *Dictionary of New Testament Theology*, "In the view of Rabbinic Judaism, the non-Israelite *gôy* is a stranger to God and far from him, counting for nothing. The Gentiles themselves are to blame for this state of affairs: they too were offered the Torah, but rejected God's instruction. They are, therefore, condemned to the judgment of hell, without hope of salvation, and have no part in the world to come. . . . God is the creator of all, but he loves Israel alone. . . .In Jewish eyes the Gentiles are unclean: they themselves, their wives and children, their houses and lands."

Daniel's Loving Respect for Unbelievers.

But the biblical record shows Daniel treating his unbelieving co-workers and supervisors with respect and a concern for their welfare. When Daniel realizes that food from the king's kitchen will contaminate him spiritually, he first takes the matter up with the "chief official." In doing so, he does not draw a my-way-or-no-way line in the sand. Instead, "he asked the chief official for permission not to defile himself" (1:8). He makes a request, not a demand. Daniel does not simply act according to his own convictions without regard for the effects on others. He belongs to an earthly community. That community has an authority structure. So he works within that structure by asking permission. Undoubtedly God uses this respectful attitude in causing the chief official "to show favor and sympathy to Daniel" (1:9).

In spite of the favor, the answer is no. So Daniel approaches the guard watching over him and his friends and asks for a ten-day test. In the NIV Daniel says, "Please test." One commentary notes that the word test is "softened by the addition of a particle, so that the resulting form is not a command but more of a polite request." Daniel's request showed courtesy. His proposal left the guard free to make his own decision, to exercise his own authority. "Treat your servants in accordance with what you see" (13), implies that Daniel and his friends will accept the decision, even if they don't get what they ask.

After hearing Nebuchadnezzar's tree dream, Daniel "was greatly perplexed for a time, and his thoughts terrified him" (4:19). The Adam Clarke commentary interprets this to mean that Daniel "felt for the king, and for the nation." And Daniel's opening statement supports this idea: "My Lord, if only the dream applied to your enemies and its meaning to your adversaries." To paraphrase, "I really don't want to have to tell you what the dream means, because its bad news will cause you and the empire a great deal of pain." Once again, Daniel shows great respect for his unbelieving boss.

Courageously, Daniel reveals the true interpretation. God will humble the proud, all-powerful Nebuchadnezzar by driving him from power. The king will look and think like an animal, live outdoors, graze like a cow and grow fingernails long and sharp as bird claws. Daniel now possesses some information he could spin into one-upmanship, or at least secret contempt. Why look up to a man whom God will put this far down? But instead, Daniel responds with healing—not cutting—words: "Therefore, O king, be pleased to accept my advice: Renounce your sins by doing what is right, and your wickedness by being kind to the oppressed. It may be that then your prosperity will continue" (4:27). For this arrogant unbelieving dictator, Daniel still seeks the best—the very definition of unselfish love. His job description did not require him to add these gracious words.

Glimpses of Jesus.

As I watch Daniel and observe his relationships with the unbelievers in his workplace, I sense that his spirit is reflecting light from a far greater source. Through Daniel's attitude toward his co-workers, I see Jesus, the friend of sinners. Daniel's example makes me think of Jesus' words to Judas who handed him over to the arresting party with a phony kiss: "Friend, do what you came for" (Matt. 26:50). In Daniel I see the same spirit as I see in Jesus as he replaces and heals the ear of Malchus, part of that same malicious gang. And in Daniel, I see the spirit that prompted the dying Jesus to pray for his unbelieving murderers—Romans as well as Jews: "Father, forgive them, for they do not know what they are doing."

Although Nebuchadnezzar is Daniel's king, he is also Daniel's workplace neighbor. In loving this arrogant boss, Daniel is doing what Jesus, hundreds of years later, would command us all to do: "Love your neighbor as yourself." Nebuchadnezzar is not only Daniel's neighbor, but also his enemy. After all, this tyrant has torn Daniel away from his family and his home and forced him to live and work in Babylon. Yet in the way he treats this enemy, Daniel gives us a glimpse of Jesus who tells us to love, bless and do good to our enemies.

Daniel's Christ-anticipating attitude toward his unbelieving boss reappears in the instructions New Testament writers penned for those in first-century workplaces—and for us. Notice how the word "respect" (emphasis added in the following Scripture quotations) becomes a theme:

- Paul writes that Christian slaves are to "be obedient to those who are your physical masters, having *respect* for them and eager concern to please them" (Eph. 6:5, Amplified Bible).
- When he reminded Timothy of what to teach those in the workplace, Paul wrote: "All who are under the yoke of slavery should consider their masters worthy of full *respect* so that God's name and our teaching may not be slandered. Those who have believing masters are not to show less *respect* for them because they are brothers" (I Tim. 6:1-2).
- Peter wrote the same kind of workplace instructions: "Slaves, submit yourselves to your masters with all *respect*, not only to those who are good and considerate, but also to those who are harsh" (I Pet. 2:18).

The words translated as "respect" in English come from various Greek terms. But they all direct us to live out the attitude we see in Daniel—even when those over us are unbelievers. If we picture love for neighbor as a beam of light shining through a prism, one of the primary colors refracted from it would be respect. Real respect is not just a veneer of niceness to cover up manipulation aimed at opening witnessing opportunities. Instead, it is genuine agape love that seeks the best for the other person.

We enjoy reading about Daniel's loving respect for his boss. We nod our agreement with Jesus' command to love our neighbors as ourselves. But the test comes as we live with those workplace neighbors day after day, week after week, year after year. Many of them and their lifestyles are not pretty. And the subtle snare for us believers is to begin thinking of ourselves—even subconsciously—as somewhat superior. Robert Ingersoll, the famous 19th century atheist, said, "Whoever imagines himself a favorite with God holds others in contempt."

Jesus had to deal with such elitism in his 12 apostles. On the way to Jerusalem, he and they needed a place to spend the night. Just one problem: they were in Samaria. Putting Jews into a Samaritan bed-and-breakfast would have been akin to inserting a metal cup into a microwave oven. In spite of this, Jesus sent some of the team on ahead to make reservations. But upon learning the party was heading for Jerusalem, the Samaritan villagers hoisted the no-vacancy sign. This snub hit a nerve in James and John. So they rushed to Jesus and proposed a plan: "Lord, do you want us to call fire down from heaven to destroy them?" (Lk. 9:54). Paraphrase: *Lord, these people don't have a clue who they're messing with. We're the God squad. We've got heaven's power. Just say the word and we'll torch the whole worthless village.* They were aiming not to show respect but to take revenge. Jesus, of course, rebuked their high-and-mighty attitude.

Paul urged Titus to teach Christians on the island of Crete how to live among unbelievers. "Remind the people to be subject to rulers and authorities, to be obedient, to be ready to do whatever is good, to slander no one, to be peaceable and considerate, and to show true humility toward all men. At one time we too were foolish, disobedient, deceived and enslaved by all kinds of passions and pleasures. We lived in malice and envy, being hated and hating one another. But when the kindness and love of God our Savior appeared, he saved us, not because of righteous things we had done, but because of his mercy" (Tit. 3:1-5). We Christians were once just as much in the dark as any unbeliever. Just because God rescued us in Christ does not make us superior to those still groping around in that darkness.

Respect Rules out Rude Witnessing.

Some of us, perhaps nurtured in traditions that make verbal witness top priority, act as if what we call the "Great Commission" trumps the second of what Jesus called the Greatest Commandments. This attitude can lead to disrespect and pushiness. Feeling intense pressure to share the Good News, the Christian may ignore signs that an unbelieving co-worker is not yet able to hear the full story of salvation. When I worked for state government, I cringed when I saw a fellow believer "witnessing" to a fellow state employee. The Christian had trapped the poor guy in the niche formed by a wall and the cold metal side of a soft-drink machine. And as his captive audience of one squirmed, the believer was giving him the full dose.

What a contrast to the instructions from Peter, who wrote: "Always be prepared to give an answer to everyone who asks you to give the reason for the hope that you have. But do this with gentleness and respect. . ." (I Pet. 3:15). There's that respect word again. Here's Peter, the bold preacher, counseling other believers to be considerate, thoughtful and caring as they explain why they've set their hope on Christ. And the explanation, Peter says, should come out of a context—in this case a door opened by the curiosity of the unbeliever. In answering the king's request to explain a dream, Daniel stepped through that open door to deliver the truth when he said, "Therefore, O king, be pleased to accept my advice: Renounce your sins by doing what is right, and your wickedness by being kind to the oppressed" (4:27).

As a Christ-follower among unbelieving co-workers, you are in a situation much like that of a Christian whose spouse has not received Christ. Just as a husband and wife share the same living space, you and your on-the-job associates must share the same working space. Like spouses, you and the non-Christians you work with must maintain a healthy relationship while you interact on a variety of issues. How are Christian wives to witness to their unbelieving husbands? Peter explains in I Peter 3:1—"Wives, in the same way be submissive to your husbands so that, if any of them do not believe the word, they may be won over without words by the behavior of their wives. . . ." This word to wives, of course, does not apply directly to the workplace. But respect and example-setting speak powerfully in both situations.

In the same passage to Christian wives, Peter urges them to present their unbelieving husbands with an inner beauty in "the way the holy women of the past who put their hope in God used to make themselves beautiful" (I Pet. 3:5). That word "beautiful" translates the Greek *kosmeo*, the root of our English word cosmetic. Paul uses the same *kosmeo* when he counsels Timothy what to teach Christian slaves about relating to their bosses. By aiming to please, refraining from back-talk and stealing, and by showing themselves trustworthy, these first-century employees were to "make the teaching about God our Savior attractive" (Tit. 2:10). By respecting unbelievers in your workplace, you beautify the gospel and make it appealing. Forceful, over-ambitious pushing distorts the gospel. The ugly caricature naturally repels.

Any legitimate work will bring along opportunities to beautify the Good News. A man I'll call Frank works for a global pharmaceutical firm as a regional sales director, a role that requires him to make life-altering, hiring/firing decisions. As a Christ-follower, Frank has found that such decisions require more than just bottom-line, profit-and-loss considerations. Into such choices he seeks to incorporate Christ's compassion.

For example, one man on his sales team was nearing retirement when the company discontinued his position. Empathizing with the man's predicament, Frank found him another position, near his home in Seattle, which would involve no cut in pay. The older man could not take the second position immediately, so Frank held it open for him. In time, after the man had begun working in his new role, it became obvious he could not adjust to the new responsibilities. This time the compassionate action meant helping the man face the truth and letting him go. Afterward, the man thanked Frank for both his caring heart and his willingness to tell him the truth.

Another of Frank's sales representatives, a reserve officer in the National Guard, was called to serve in Iraq. Frank's company had no policy about holding positions open for those who had to leave for military deployment. In spite of this, Frank pledged to the soldier that his job would be waiting for him upon his return after 18 months. This sales rep had been responsible for one of the larger territories in Frank's region, so Frank had to sell this potentially costly commitment to his sales manager.

A year-and-a-half later, when the man returned, he shook Frank's hand, pressing into it a coin-like disk. One side carried an army reserve emblem and the other side an outline map of Iraq along with the name of the mission just finished. "Thank you," said the soldier. "You have no idea what it meant to me and my family to have no worries about my coming back to a job. So many bosses of my fellow soldiers simply don't live by your standards." A year after his return from Iraq, the company recognized this reinstated sales representative for being in the top one-percent globally in total sales. The man still sends Frank a thank-you card every year.

Frank in his work, like Daniel in his, is reflecting the Spirit of Christ as he relates to his work-neighbors with respect.

Sometimes respect means we Christians need to change our ways. Heather worked as one of three bankruptcy paralegals in a small office of five people. One of the other paralegals was a Christian; the other was not. "When the non-Christian paralegal first began working with me," Heather says, "she let me know that some of my word choices irritated her. I had a habit of describing something that annoyed me as 'retarded.' For example, if a TV ad offended me, I'd refer to it as 'such a retarded commercial.' After my co-worker objected to my language, I told her I'd stop using the word. She told me that wouldn't be necessary, but I recognized how much it bothered her and wanted to show her I cared about her.

"I didn't see this as spreading the gospel, but as trying to show God's love to an unbeliever through my actions. And I wanted to avoid giving her any reason to dislike or avoid Christians or Christ, since I had made it clear to her that I was a believer. She quickly noticed and appreciated the change. So far I've succeeded in eliminating that adjective from my vocabulary—and she and I have become good friends. We still have all kinds of discussions about God and Jesus and life. I continue to pray that God will give me wisdom as we talk and that she will accept him as Lord of her life."

Heather—like Frank and Daniel—did not just love her co-worker "with words or tongue but with actions and in truth" (I Jn. 3:18).

Respect Requires Attentive Listening.

The book of Daniel lets us eavesdrop on several of Daniel's interactions with unbelieving co-workers. He listened as King Nebuchadnezzar spelled out what he wanted Daniel to do. He listened as the same king retold a rather complex dream. He listened as King Belshazzar asked him to read the mysterious writing on the wall. Even as he sat in the lions' den, Daniel listened as he let King Darius have the first word. Each time, Daniel had an opportunity to speak, but it came after and as a result of his careful listening.

Convinced that we are to evangelize, many of us Christians take that to mean relying mainly on our words and tongues in dealing with unbelievers. We would do well, though, to listen to what they're saying about us. In a blog with the title, "Why I Don't Want to be a Christian," the author wrote: "Christians have formed two levels of cliques. There is the Christian clique, which you are in when you've accepted Jesus Christ as your personal Savior. With this clique you are either in or out. If you're in, then you are treated as an individual who is overall good. If you're out, then you are always trying to be brought in through clever Christian sales pitches. Then there are the cliques within the larger Christian clique. These are known as denominations. Even though Christians claim to be inviting and accepting of all, they take up arms against other so-called brothers and sisters in Christ."

Unbelievers in the work world have built up an immunity to "clever Christian sales pitches." Even as I was writing these words, two men from a cult knocked on our door. Rather than listening, one of them began with an obviously canned lead sentence about how everyone these days is worried about the economy. Anyone could have seen through the hidden agenda. The word "pitchman" describes a high-pressure salesperson, and may call to mind the words David Segal, a Washington Post staff writer, used to describe a TV pitchman: "bellowing like a man who thinks that the whole world has gone a little deaf." True, the unbelieving world has gone deaf to the gospel. But while shouting may add sizzle to selling gizmos on TV, it does not cure spiritual deafness. Could it be that some of the world's deafness results from our unwillingness to listen?

Joining God in His Work.

In his widely used study, *Experiencing God*, Henry Blackaby urges believers to discover where God is working and then to join him in it. That's precisely what Daniel did when Nebuchadnezzar asked for help with his troubling tree dream. God had already been at work in giving the king a dream full of meaning. For Nebuchadnezzar, his dream created a crisis. In the king's own words, "I had a dream that made me afraid" (4:5). His God-given dream disrupted his peaceful palace life and triggered emotional instability and uncertainty. Daniel joined God in his crisis-causing work by explaining to the king what it all meant.

Those in your work circles will also face crises as their life stories unfold. On coffee breaks, through small talk, the workplace grapevine and in many other ways you'll learn of all kinds of predicaments and emergencies. Gene asks for sick leave to undergo surgery for prostate cancer. Jennifer and her husband have just separated. Your assistant can't concentrate because her teenaged son spent the night in jail on drug charges. The crises show up in every area of life. Overwhelming credit card debt. Broken interpersonal relationships. Discrimination. Job loss. Bankruptcy. You won't be able to step into every situation—nor should you. But if you remain sensitive to what's happening in the lives of those around you at work, you may discover that God is at work in this or that devastating circumstance. And it may be that God will direct you, as he did Daniel, to help a co-worker see the divine hand at work.

Loving respect won Daniel the right to speak—without becoming a pitchman—some appropriate words of witness to his boss. Through Daniel, the prideful King Nebuchadnezzar heard what he most needed to hear: ". . . the Most High is sovereign over the kingdoms of men and gives them to anyone he wishes" (4:25). In your workplace, loving respect will open doors of opportunity to speak, doors that have been dead-bolted against other approaches. But it must be genuine love and real respect.

Workplace ministry to unbelievers, unlike a church program, cannot be conveniently scheduled. It will happen on God's timetable, not yours. The results of this kind of ministry typically resist measurement and demand long-term commitment. To sustain such a ministry requires more than merely human grit and determination. You'll need resources that come only from that unseen "river whose streams make glad the city of God, the holy place where the Most High dwells" (Ps. 46:4). The chapters in Part Three will explore how Daniel tapped into that river.

PUTTING IT TO WORK

- Look again at the descriptions of the six work associates in the bulleted list that opens this chapter. Then honestly answer the questions that follow the list: How do you treat them? How do you secretly view them? Would you eat lunch with them? Invite them into your home? Do you judge them? Tolerate them? Try to avoid them?

- What did your answers reveal about your own attitude toward and relationship with unbelievers?
- In what ways do you see Jesus reflected in the way Daniel treated his unbelieving co-workers?
- How has God used you or other Christians in your workplace to touch the lives of unbelievers around you?
- Which of the non-Christians in your workplace are facing difficulties that God may be using in the process of drawing them to faith in Christ? What are those difficulties? How might you respond?

PART

FINDING STRENGTH TO GO ON

A runner in the 105th Boston Marathon described her ordeal in these words: "I strode confidently through the first half, passing the 13-mile mark in under two hours. And then, at mile 15, I started to realize that I might have a problem. The weather was unusually warm, and I had not prepared for it. Dressed in my winter leggings, I was hot and couldn't shed another layer. At mile 18, I hit the wall. I can only describe hitting the wall in one way: pain, pain, and more pain. Every muscle in my body ached and was screaming at me to stop."

Christians in the marathon of a career in the work world can also hit the wall. "Believer-friendly" hardly describes Babylon in Daniel's day. Nor does the term fit the "Babylon" of today's world-system. As a Christ-follower, you won't find your natural habitat in the world's workplaces. Like Daniel, you're an alien. A stranger. A citizen from another kingdom. "Babylon" represents confusion, the world-system organized apart from and even against God. Daniel fought the good fight, kept the faith and finished the race in the pagan work world of his day. Part Three surveys Daniel's life to uncover the inner resources that made him able not only to survive but to thrive in his long career in Babylon.

Chapter Nine probes for clues about his faith. What did he

count on God to be and to do? How did he keep going without the religious support system he had known back in Jerusalem? Daniel's worship forms the focal point of Chapter Ten. What did worship mean to him? Why was he able to offer his everyday work as worship? Why do so many Christians today find work-as-worship so difficult? Chapter Eleven observes how Daniel practiced spiritual disciplines. How did he train himself in godliness? What can we, 27 centuries later, learn from his exercises to stay spiritually fit? And finally, Chapter Twelve explores where he found his power to bear fruit and to finish well.

In New York City's 2008 marathon more than 38,000 finished the course. But 416 runners dropped out. Most dropouts had physical reasons for quitting: overheating, dehydration, injuries, insufficient training or whatever. Not all who begin the spiritual marathon of the workplace finish well. But with coaching from Daniel, who knew how to tap the resources of God's eternal kingdom, you can find the strength to persevere.

FAITH: TRUSTING GOD SOLO

". . . without faith it is impossible to please God. . . ."
    Heb. 11:6

"Surrounded by a world that carried none of the comfortable signs of the religious life, I slowly began to discover that Christ stands at the center of our life in the world where we expend most of our time and expertise. I found that he is, indeed, Lord of the world. . . ."
    Richard Broholm, "How Can You Believe You're a Minister When the Church Keeps Telling You You're Not?"
    (a chapter in the book, *The Laity in Ministry*)

Framing the Issue: According to a county extension agent, "Trees growing in groups survived hurricane winds better . . . than those standing individually." Like trees, believers can find protection in groups. But no group can exercise faith for you. Your work will often require you to stand by yourself against strong winds of opposition. Daniel, though bolstered by his small group of believers, models the importance of personal faith in facing workplace storms on your own.

He was just a kid. Maybe 13. Or 17. Suddenly in Babylon, everything had changed for him. Here, none of the religious guardrails of Judaism protected him from hazards along his path. No temple. No priests. No sacrifices. No Sabbaths on the Babylonian calendar. Then, as we saw in Chapter Two, he faced his first crisis without all those supports. The meals provided for him and the other apprentices veered outside the dietary boundaries ingrained in him since infancy. What to do? Simply go along? After all, neither his parents nor the High Priest would ever find out he'd eaten non-kosher food. Why should he refrain when his king, his supervisors and the non-Jewish trainees would all endorse a decision to eat up and enjoy? Why should he abstain? Just one reason: *his faith*. Right from the start of his career in Babylon, this teenager found his way to a diet that would not pollute him spiritually. And he did so *through faith*.

This word *faith*, one of the most frequent and important words in the Bible, never appears in the Book of Daniel. Nor do the words *believe, believed, belief* or *believing*. Hebrews 11, often called the "faith chapter," does not mention Daniel by name. But he's certainly there as the one who "through faith . . . shut the mouths of lions" (11:33). In Daniel, then, we don't find an academic definition of faith. Daniel does not set out to parse faith in terms of its Hebrew usage in the Old Testament. Instead, Daniel—anticipating what James would write hundreds of years later—seems to be saying, "I will show you my faith by what I do" (Jas. 2:18).

Daniel's Workplace Faith.

The word *trusted,* which occurs twice in the Book of Daniel, illustrates faith on display as doing. Both times *trusted* explains an action taken in the context of a job-related situation. In the first case Nebuchadnezzar, in clarifying why Daniel's three friends had refused to carry out the boss's order to bow to an idol, says, "They trusted in him [God] and defied the king's command" (3:28). In the second case the text tells why Daniel came out of the lions' den with no wounds—"because he had trusted in his God" (6:23). Throughout the entire book of Daniel, in one workplace incident after another, Daniel's faith shows through in action rather than in detailed definitions and abstractions.

Let's look again at Nebuchadnezzar's dream in Daniel 2, this time from the faith angle. Can you imagine what it took for Daniel to stand in front of the most powerful man in the world after that man had issued an executive order for his execution? As Daniel stands there he knows that the king has had a dream. Although the king has no idea what the dream means, he remembers its plot line perfectly. He will reverse the death penalty only if someone can narrate it exactly. Get one detail wrong and it's all over. Just a short time before this appearance before the king, Daniel has been on the king's hunt-down-and-kill list. Try to picture the expression on this proud king's face as he asks Daniel, "Are you sure you can do this—tell me the dream I had and interpret it for me" (2:26, *The Message*)?

Faith that God Exists. Right off, Daniel admits that no mere human expert can do what the king is asking. "But," he quickly adds, "there is a God in heaven who reveals mysteries" (2:28). Nebuchadnezzar believed in "gods," just as his astrologers did (2:11). But those gods could not reveal this dream or any other mystery. In saying, "there is a God in heaven," Daniel bears witness to his faith in the existence of the God who is over all. No wonder Daniel would later make it into the "faith chapter." As the writer of Hebrews puts it, "anyone who comes to him [God] must believe that he exists and that he rewards those who earnestly seek him" (Heb. 11:6). In a delicate, risk-filled encounter with his boss, Daniel's speech makes his faith visible: he hangs his entire fate on his faith that the God in heaven does in fact exist.

Faith that God Rewards. We've seen that before this meeting with the king, Daniel and his friends had prayed about the job-related crisis. In doing so, they demonstrated their faith that this God of heaven "rewards those who earnestly seek him." And God did reward their prayers of faith. Afterward, in his praise and thanks, Daniel said, ". . . you have made known to me what we asked of you, you have made known to us the dream of the king" (2:23).

Workplace issues, then, showed that Daniel's faith met the two basic faith-standards found in Hebrews 11:6. One, he believed God exists. And two, he believed this God rewards those who seriously seek him. As the Book of Daniel proceeds, what Daniel says and does in response to several other workplace situations give us even further insight into his faith. We will look at these in the order they appear.

Faith that God Reveals. As Daniel confessed his faith that God exists (2:28), he also makes it clear he believes in the God who reveals. In speaking with his boss, Daniel even calls God the "revealer of mysteries" (2:29). So the God Daniel believed in not only exists and rewards, he also reveals. In contrast to the deaf and dumb gods of the Babylonians, he is God the Communicator. As Daniel found, God communicates not just with priests and religious professionals, but with believers who spend their days and years in non-religious jobs.

I once worked for a small state agency that had lost its director. With the staff accountable to no one, chaos soon ruled. In discussing the situation with a retired colonel who had come to work for the agency, I suggested that we pray for wisdom about what to do. He snorted and said, "Prayer? I don't think it's come to that!" Sometimes even Christians act as if God reveals things only in a religious context but not in the ordinary world of work. Or to guard the term "revelation," we limit it to what God said to those who wrote Scripture. Of course, Scripture is our unique source of God's special revelation to give us salvation wisdom. Scripture is our "only rule for faith and practice." But Scripture itself tells us that God put human beings here to rule the earth under his direction. So is it too much to believe that he unfolds insight and wisdom to those who, through their jobs, work to bring that part of his creation into line with his will?

The scientist George Washington Carver, a Christian, found 300 ways to use peanuts. He discovered many other roles for soybeans, sweet potatoes and pecans. Products from these plants included adhesives, bleach, chili sauce and ink—to name just a few. Carver relied on God to uncover what he needed to know about plants for the benefit of God's world. He said, "God is going to reveal to us things He never revealed before if we put our hands in His." He also said, "I love to think of nature as an unlimited broadcasting station, through which God speaks to us every hour, if we will only tune in." You serve the same God as Daniel and George Washington Carver. What might God want to reveal to and through you concerning your work?

Faith that God Rules. In his interpretation of Nebuchadnezzar's tree dream, Daniel tells the king he will remain in his cut-down state until he recognizes "that the Most High is sovereign over the kingdoms of men" (4:25). Nebuchadnezzar will be raised back up again only when he acknowledges that "Heaven rules" (4:26). His faith that God rules made Daniel able to keep even the most powerful workplace supervisor in perspective. None of his bosses had ultimate authority. Each of them operated under the overarching rule of God.

The hierarchies in charge of corporate workplaces sometimes seem all-powerful. From your cubicle, you may feel helpless against the decisions being made by people "up there" whom you can neither see nor hear. In my final years as a state employee, I served in an "exempt" position. Even though I belonged to neither political party, that meant I served at the pleasure of the governor. After I had worked in the administration of one governor for 11 years, he decided not to run for re-election. This time the voters chose a governor from the opposite political party. She decided to fire all of us exempts. Was the end of my job a tragic loss—something outside God's sovereignty? Not at all. Losing my job motivated me to start a business of my own, a decision God clearly blessed as the years passed. I found, as Daniel had, that "the Most High is sovereign over the kingdoms of men." Believing in the sovereign God, you can rely on the promise in Romans 8:28, "And we know that in all things God works for the good of those who love him, who have been called according to his purpose."

Faith that God Sees. Daniel is probably around 80 years old in Chapter 5. He may be retired—or in some lower-level job. At any rate, the new king, Belshazzar, does not know him. When the mysterious hand writes on the wall, the king nearly faints. Just in time a queen old enough to remember Daniel enters the room and tells about his unique gift of unscrambling obscure messages. So the king summons the old man and offers rewards if he can interpret the cryptic message on the wall. Daniel reminds the king how the proud Nebuchadnezzar had learned the hard way about God's sovereign rule. Belshazzar, though he had known those facts, refused to humble himself. Instead, he worshiped false gods who could not see, hear or understand. Now, through the printing in the plaster, he was about to learn that the true God is not blind. He has been watching every detail of this arrogance. He is, Daniel says, "the God who holds in his hand your life and all your ways" (5:23). Daniel's faith in the God who sees explains why Daniel worked with such integrity that even his enemies could not find fault with it.

In normal times, the labor force in the United States totals roughly 150 million. Suppose the average working person averages one decision on an ethical question each day. That would amount to 150 million right-versus-wrong choices in the workplace daily. Let's say half of these people believe God sees each choice and why they make it. The other half think God can't or doesn't bother to see such things. Each group will be making 75 million ethical decisions per day. How do you think the choices of the God-sees group would differ from the God-doesn't-see group? Which workers would do a better job of ruling their small corner of the earth by bringing situations into line with God's will? When you approach your job with Daniel's kind of faith, you know that God sees each choice you make in your workplace. "Nothing in all creation is hidden from God's sight" (Heb. 4:13).

Faith that God Rescues. In Daniel's best-known workplace incident, the lions' den, yet another aspect of his faith shines through. Dumped into the death trap because he stayed true to God in spite of treacherous co-workers, Daniel spent the night among the lions. In the morning, his king (this time King Darius) rushes to the den and anxiously asks: "Daniel, servant of the living God, has your God, whom you serve continually, been able to rescue you from the lions" (6:20)? Daniel—still alive and able to answer—calls back, "My God sent his angel, and he shut the mouths of the lions" (6:22). Then the text goes on to explain that "no wound was found on him, because he had trusted in his God" (6:23). The real God who exists, Daniel firmly believed, is the God who also rescues. And because of this faith, Daniel was able to face whatever came up in his workplace without flinching or giving in to fear.

Faith in the God who rescues does not lead to the naïve idea that he will always snag us out of every danger zone. Daniel's friends, Shadrach, Meshach and Abednego, said it best in refusing to bow to the king's golden idol. After threatening them with being cremated alive in a blazing furnace, the king asked, "Then what god will be able to rescue you from my hand" (3:15). Their answer rings with real faith: "If we are thrown into the blazing furnace, the God we serve is able to save us from it, and he will rescue us from your hand, O king. But even if he does not, we want you to know, O king, that we will not serve your gods or worship the image of gold you have set up" (3:17-18). The sovereign God is always *able* to rescue you. Whether he is *willing* to rescue you in this or that workplace crisis is another matter.

Faith that God Forgives. In light of Daniel's remarkable life, it would be easy to idealize him into some faultless demigod. But Daniel did not see himself that way. In his prayer in Chapter 9, he includes himself in the "we" of confession. "We have sinned and done wrong" (v. 5). "We have not listened to your servants the prophets" (v. 6). "We are covered with shame" (v. 7). And so on. In verse 20, Daniel admits to personal failures when he speaks of "confessing my sin." How did he handle his guilt? He could not go to the Temple and ask a priest to sacrifice a lamb or a bull for his sins. But in 9:9, Daniel shows another aspect of his faith: "The Lord our God is merciful and forgiving." And because he believed in the God who cancels human sin, Daniel asks in v. 19, "O Lord, forgive!" Daniel was not paralyzed by whatever failures may have marred his performance in the workplace. He did not remain groveling in guilt. The past and its shortfalls did not keep him from pressing on, because he believed in the God who forgives.

Being a Christian in your workplace does not mean you'll never miss the mark or fall short. Nor does it mean that your influence as a believer is done for because co-workers know you've failed. The Christian faith is not perfectionism. Your witness does not depend on your never ever doing anything wrong. Instead, you glorify God when—as one struggling against sin—you drag what you've said or done into his light, confess it and rest in his promise of forgiveness because of Christ's death in your place. Confident of God's pardon, you are then able to admit your failures to others affected by it and to take whatever steps may be needed to restore right relationships with them. Your faith is not in your own flawless walk but in the God of Daniel, the God who forgives.

Your Workplace Faith.

Faith is faith, whether you're in a Bible study group, at home with the family or working on a project in the office or shop. But faith in the workplace requires the kind of rugged stamina we see in

Daniel's example. In a gathered-church setting, you exercise faith surrounded by a support group. Those fellow believers are pulling for you. The same goes at home if you're blessed with a Christian family. But on the job, chances are you're mostly encircled by people who don't share your faith in Christ. Don't fight it. This is just the way Jesus planned it. Remember, he told his first disciples, "I am sending you out like lambs among wolves" (Lk. 10:3).

Further, you exercise faith at work without the propping-up effect of an ecclesiastical title. A friend of mine has worked both with and without those external supports. She first served as a nurse and then as a computer programmer for the U. S. Navy. After learning of an opening in cross-cultural mission work in Bangkok, Thailand, she applied and the mission organization accepted her. "Once I let Christians know I was headed for Bangkok," she recalls, "I suddenly began receiving frequent invitations to speak. Now that I carried the label 'missionary,' they just assumed I had something to say worth listening to. This surprised me, because the mission board hired me for the same skills I had been using in so-called 'secular' work. Christians placed me on a pedestal because I was willing to 'sacrifice and suffer' as a missionary. I felt hypocritical, because for me my work required neither. As long as I was engaged in foreign mission work, Christians showed keen interest in what I was doing. People constantly asked how they could pray for me and my work."

For the next six-and-one-half years she served first in Thailand, then in Laos, as an administrator in relief and development work. But when she returned to work in the States, the letter-writers stopped asking about her work. The prayer support ended. "I was still doing the same things here as I had been doing there," she says. "Back in the States, working for the government, I was still engaged in serving God full-time. But now I experienced mostly an absence of interest in my work. I felt demoted."

Daniel was not a chaplain to the government employees in Babylon. He had not come as a recognized missionary backed by a sending board back home. He was not Reverend, Father or Pastor Daniel. Just Daniel (or maybe "Shaz," if that was short for Belteshazzar). In other words, he was not in the workplace to carry out the duties even the world expects of a professional clergyperson. Nor did he enjoy the formal respect and perks that come with such roles. Like Daniel, you will draw staying-power not through religious rank or privilege but solely through your faith in God.

As you work, you have no pastor or board of elders looking over your shoulder to hold you accountable. No one among your co-workers will enforce any church bylaws or membership covenants. Why, then, should you refrain from gossip? Why not fudge on the expense report? What's stopping you from promising potential customers more than the product or service can really deliver? Just one reason: *your faith.* The consciousness that you are living every day of your life under the loving yet watchful eye of the sovereign God who is shaping history.

As we've seen, Daniel made it into the Heb. 11 hall of fame as one who by faith "shut the mouths of lions." He, like many in that chapter, saw God work in spectacular, triumphant ways. Others went through beatings, prison sentences, stoning and dismemberment without God's miraculous intervention. But the chapter twice makes the point that none of them—neither the "winners" nor the "losers"—received everything God had promised them (Heb. 11:13, 39). They all died "still living by faith." The very last words in the Book of Daniel, spoken by the man clothed in linen, assured Daniel that he would die, "then at the end of the days you will rise to receive your allotted inheritance." Daniel, too, died in faith still waiting for the full measure of what God had promised him.

Should You Expect to Change the World?

In this, Daniel's experience reflects yet another fact about your faith in the workplace: *don't expect complete fulfillment during your earthly lifetime.* David prayed that God would deliver him from wicked people, "men of this world whose reward is in this life" (Ps. 17:14). Among Christians today, it has become popular to believe, "You can change your world." Christian colleges recruit students with this slogan. One fairly recent graduate of a Christian school wrote: "I want to leave the world a better place than I found it. Tough assignment, but worth a try."

We're focusing on faith in this chapter. Faith trusts God and his promises. So when I hear or read this slogan, "You can change the world," I ask: has God ever commissioned Christians to change the world? Has he promised that he will use us in that way? Or, looking again at Daniel, was the world different as a result of his work in Babylon? When you go to work tomorrow morning, does God send you there to change the world?

This question raises another: In the slogan, "You can change the world," what does the word *world* mean? In the New Testament, the usual Greek word for world is *kosmos* (from which we get words like cosmetic, cosmic and cosmopolitan). At root, the word refers to a harmonious, orderly arrangement—one that adorns or beautifies. In various New Testament contexts *kosmos* carries four basic meanings:

- The physical creation. The harmonious universe created by God. "The God who made the world . . ." (Acts 17:24).
- The human population of the earth. "For God so loved the world . . ." (Jn. 3:16).
- The world's human population alienated from and hostile to God. "If the world hates you, keep in mind that it hated me first" (Jn. 15:18).
- The worldly system organized around temporal concerns without any accountability to God. It includes world-oriented possessions, positions and pleasures. "Do not love the world or anything in the world" (I Jn. 2:15).

The answer to the question, "Can you change the world?" depends, then, on which "world" you mean. If you refer to meaning #1, the physical creation, the answer is yes. God commissioned the human race to rule over and subdue the earth. So when George Washington Carver discovered how to subdue the peanut, part of physical creation, so that it would serve people in new ways, he was changing the world in that sense.

If "world" means #2 or #3, the human population of the earth, the question really means, can you change people? Like Daniel, we can certainly set an example that influences them. We can witness to them by telling them God's revealed truth about sin and salvation. We can encourage, counsel, warn and pray for them. But only God can change human hearts. If we caution newly married couples against trying to change each other, can we expect to change the human population of the world?

When it comes to meaning #4, the worldly system organized against God and his kingdom, the answer seems obvious. This world-system, created and headed by Satan himself, will continue to oppose God until "the kingdom of this world has become the kingdom of our Lord and of his Christ" (Rev. 11:15). Daniel didn't change the world-system. The prophecies God revealed through him foretold the coming of one corrupt ruler after another long after Daniel's days on earth. Trying to change the world system would be like trying to change gravel into gold. No amount of negotiation with the ruler of this world will change his mind or his hostility to God.

My point is this: *If you believe that, through your daily work, you can change the world's human population or its anti-God system, you may be setting yourself up for great disappointment.* You might reach the end of your career only to look back and see that your faith aimed for an impossible target.

What Should You Expect Your Work to Do?

If we believers are not here to change to the world in the last three ways, what *can* you purpose—in faith—to accomplish as you work in the world?

First, God can use your work to rule over and subdue his physical creation in ways that brings it into line with his agenda—so that his will is done here on earth as it is in heaven. For example, your work might help discover how to increase crop yields, subduing the earth to feed more people more efficiently. Or your work might contribute to the tapping or distributing of earth's energy resources for the benefit of everyone.

Second, through your work you can obey the greatest commandments—to love God and to love your neighbor. Legitimate work, whatever it may be, provides a service. In this way, through your daily work you exercise your "faith expressing itself through love" (Gal. 5:6). You can illustrate this from your own work, whether your field is child-care, clothing, education, food, government, health care, manufacturing or what have you. Daniel worked in government administration, helping to keep order for the benefit of people throughout an empire.

Third, by faith you can through your work reflect the image of God and embody the truth as it is in Jesus. Through Daniel, light from heaven penetrated the darkness of Babylon. God used his faithfulness to the truth to humble the proud Nebuchadnezzar and to demonstrate—even to unbelieving co-workers—what God intended a human being to be and to do. Jesus calls us Christians to be his witnesses, by what we are, say and do, in the whole world—including the work world. In that world, people typically place their faith in themselves, in hard work, in education or in just plain luck. If you, following Daniel's lead, work from a platform of faith in the sovereign God, your work will stand out in sharp contrast to most of those around you.

Daniel learned to gaze on God through the eyes of faith.

What he saw transformed him in profound ways and led him to worship. In our day, work and worship may seem to belong in separate compartments. But Daniel knew they belonged together. As Chapter Ten will show, the way he understood and practiced worship can bring a whole new dimension to your daily work.

PUTTING IT TO WORK

- What to you is the most encouraging example of Daniel displaying his faith through situations that came up in the course of his daily work?
- Give one or two examples of how you have demonstrated your faith in God by means of your actions in the workplace.
- In your own experience, how might exercising faith while in a church crowd differ from exercising faith in your workplace? What additional pressures does faith in the workplace involve?
- From what you have observed, where are your non-Christian co-workers placing their faith? (Think in terms of persons, systems, beliefs, finances, dreams and so on.)
- Do you agree or disagree with what this chapter says about changing the world? Explain your answer.

CHAPTER TEN

WORSHIP: SERVING GOD IN AWE

"Work and worship are rarely connected in the lives and minds of most Christians."
Luke Bretherton, "Work as Worship"

"Seemingly secular works are a worship of God and an obedience well pleasing to God."
Martin Luther

"If the people of God are to be freed for ministry in the workplace, worship will need to be viewed as involving the whole of life and not just Sunday morning."
Ray Bystrom, "Ten Words for Those Who Work: Worship"

Framing the Issue: We Christians have come to associate "worship" almost exclusively with our weekend gatherings. Worship *leaders.* Worship *teams.* Worship *style.* Worship *service.* Worship *center.* None of these terms connects with the work we do the rest of the week. So our very vocabulary helps to distance work from worship. What God's Word joins together, we have separated. By his example, Daniel shows us how to reunite our worship with our work.

We contemporary Christians have invented an expression I'm sure Daniel never heard—the term "worship wars." A Google search, with quotation marks to limit it to those two words, turned up nearly 23,000 hits. Right off, the two words ram against each other like linemen on opposing football teams. Worship takes adoration; war takes ammunition. Worship is awe; war is awful. Worship produces rest and peace; war generates conflict and chaos. So how could real worship ever bring siblings in Christ to civil war?

Almost always these wars break out over the way to do music in church meetings. The battles typically erupt over hymns versus praise choruses, organs as opposed to guitars, or choirs against worship teams. One pastor was heard to say, "If these drums go, I go." The fact that music usually sets off these skirmishes points to something else we up-to-date Christians have done with the word *worship*. We've come close to redefining it as corporate singing.

But biblically the word *worship* does not trace its meaning to music. Bible words translated as worship often describe bodily actions that demonstrate reverence or honor. Old Testament Hebrew words speak of bowing the head, bending the knees or falling prostrate. New Testament words for worship include terms that mean kissing the hand or ground—each requiring one to bow. These terms grew from visible bodily motions that display the unseen worship of the heart or spirit. A. W. Tozer once defined worship as, "A humbling but delightful sense of admiring awe and astonished wonder." Yes, we can express worship through music, but also in many other ways. Daniel remained a worshiper of God throughout his career as a busy bureaucrat. He may have included music and singing as a part of his worship, but the Bible does not say so.

Centuries of tradition have also conditioned us to connect worship with "sacred" space. Many still describe church buildings as "the house of God." Some refer to the facility they meet in as their "worship center." Although his ancestors had worshiped in the Jerusalem Temple for hundreds of years, Daniel's worship did not depend on his being in some holy space. He lacked those things many today might consider essential for worshiping God. But the story of his life leaves no question that he worshiped, as Jesus would later put it, "in spirit and in truth."

Worship During Off-Hours.

Daniel 6 shows that he had a well-established pattern of praying. Where did he pray? In his upstairs room, his ordinary living space. When did he pray? Three times a day. Why three? The text doesn't say. He certainly knew the Psalms, so he may have taken his cue from Ps. 55:17—"Evening, morning and noon I cry out in distress, and he hears my voice." How did he pray? "On his knees," his body-language reflecting the fact that his heart had taken the low place before the awesome God. What did he pray? He was "giving thanks to his God" and "asking God for help" (6:10, 11).

Chapter 9 gives us even more insight into Daniel the worshiper. Reading the Scriptures apparently prompted this prayer (9:2). The opening sentence focuses not on Daniel but on the Deity and his breathtaking *immensity*: "O Lord, the great and awesome God" (9:4). Don't rush over that first single-syllable, single-letter word. Small, yes, but so significant. To quote Tozer once more, "We Christians should watch lest we lose the 'Oh!' from our hearts." Daniel then remembers God's *faithfulness*, the God "who keeps his covenant of love with all who love him and obey his commands." In verse 7 Daniel shifts his gaze to God's *moral perfection*: "Lord, you are righteous." The remembrance of God's history of dealing with his people stirs his worship: "O Lord our God, who brought your people out of Egypt with a mighty hand and made a name for yourself that endures to this day" (9:15). In the rest of this prayer, he praises God for his *compassion*, his *power* and his *renown*. As we eavesdrop on Daniel at prayer, we see that his worship flows in an artesian stream from what he sees as he fastens the eyes of his heart and mind on God.

Daniel's worship merges with confession. As he contemplates the holy, infinite God, Daniel can't help but notice the stark contrast. Seeing God's majesty and holiness inevitably draws attention to his and his fellow Israelites' spiritual poverty. Worship shrivels the ego. Worship leads him to confess his own sin and the sins of his people (9:20). Though Daniel is praying as an individual ("I prayed," 9:4), he prays with a group awareness. Even alone, he knows his solidarity with a body of people. Neither his confession nor his worship is individualistic. If I counted right, in this one prayer he uses the plural pronoun "we" 16 times, "our" 17 times and "us" 8 times. Centuries later, in modeling prayer for his followers, Jesus also filled his example with plural pronouns. "Give *us* today *our* daily bread. Forgive *us* our debts, as *we* also have forgiven *our* debtors. And lead *us* not into temptation, but deliver *us* from the evil one."

Watching this bureaucrat from Babylon offers valuable insights for Christians in today's work world. His example makes it clear that authentic worship can take place without worship teams, amplifiers, PowerPoint slides, pianos, keyboards, drums, organs or guitars, hymns or choruses. None of the issues that incite the worship wars had anything to do with Daniel's capacity to stand in awe of God. Nor did Daniel's worship require a spiritually sanitized space. In his experience, he anticipated what Jesus would tell the Samaritan woman at the well: "…a time is coming when you will worship the Father neither on this mountain [the sacred space for Samaritans] nor in Jerusalem [the sacred space for Jews]. . . .a time is coming and has now come when the true worshipers will worship the Father in spirit and truth, for they are the kind of worshipers the Father seeks." (Jn. 4:21, 23). Even if you're embroiled in one of today's demanding work schedules, you can worship God at home, in your car, your office or your shop. How? By fixing your gaze on Jesus and, seeing Daniel's God, letting praise flow spontaneously from your heart and mouth.

Worship While You Work.

But Daniel's worship extended far beyond praying three-times-a-day (or even more). He also worshiped God as he worked for Nebuchadnezzar, for Belshazzar and for Darius. His work may have meant drafting a Babylonian public works budget. Or arranging for the training of the newest cream-of-the-crop captives. Or ghost-writing official letters for the king. Whatever his work, Daniel would have understood that he could offer it, too, as acceptable worship to his God.

How do I know Daniel would have understood work as acceptable worship? Because of the Hebrew Bible that had shaped him from boyhood. The Hebrew words *avad* and its offspring, *avodah*, appear nearly 450 times in the Old Testament. In English, they typically translate into *work, worship* and *service*. For example:

- "The Lord God took the man and put him in the Garden of Eden to **work (avad)** it and take care of it" (Gen. 2:15).
- "When you have brought the people out of Egypt, you will **worship (avad)** God on this mountain" (Ex. 3:12).
- "Six days you shall labor and do all your **work (avad)**" (Ex. 20:9).
- "Let my people go, so that they may **worship (avad)** me" (Ex. 8:1).
- I am giving you the **service (avodah)** of the priesthood as a gift" (Num. 18:7).
- "Fear the Lord your God, **serve (avad)** him only and take your oaths in his name" (Deut. 6:13; quoted by Jesus in Matt. 4:10 after the devil asked for his worship).

Mike Metzger of the Clapham Institute recommends a simple experiment to demonstrate why contemporary attempts to "integrate faith and work" usually don't work. He suggests asking others to sketch pictures that show what they think when they hear the words *worship, work, ministry, the arts* and *service.* Metzger says, "From my experience, people draw five different pictures—something like *hands raised* for worship, a *computer* for work, *people with other people* for ministry, *musical notes or paint brushes* for the arts and *people helping people* for service. Yet the reality is that throughout the Old Testament, one word—*'avodah'*—is translated as *worship, work, ministry, the arts* and *service.* . . . God sees all five as threads in a seamless fabric labeled *avodah.* . . .He didn't cut three fabrics—one for religious people, one for business professionals and one for weirdos with orange hair. The fabric of avodah means there is no such thing as 'full-time Christian work'—unless we include the butcher, baker and candlestick maker along with monks, missionaries and clergy. *All* work is worship when done as it *ought to be.* . . ."

Two Questions.

Metzger's "seamless fabric" observations raise two questions. First, why could the Jews describe both work and worship in the same word? Second, why do we Christians today have such a hard time seeing how we could possibly offer our work to God as worship? Let's explore those questions one at a time.

Why One Word for Work and Worship? The answer to the first question can be summed up in one word: *service.* The Hebrew Bible Daniel read presented both work and worship as *service.* Each, when offered to God, served him. Daniel saw no sacred-secular dividing line between his day job and his worship. To him, it was all *avad,* all serving God, all worship.

Daniel knew the biblical story of creation. In that account, the God who made the earth deputized the human beings he had formed from its dust. They were to "rule . . . over all the earth," including its creatures (Gen. 1:26)—the whole planet! When God placed man in the Garden of Eden, he was "to work it and take care of it" (Gen. 2:15). The entire earth belonged to God because he had created it. God would carry out his purposes on the stage of the earth—and man was to serve him as the "stage crew," maintaining it so that those purposes could be acted out on it. The immensity of the earth-stage means that the work of managing it requires a great many diverse activities: *agriculture, transportation, government, health care, education, environment, information, law, manufacturing, protection* and *sanitation*, to name just a few major ones.

In chapter 8, Daniel sees a vision. The angel Gabriel comes to explain what it all means. The interpretation actually makes Daniel so ill he needs several days of bed rest. Imagine filling your sick leave report and explaining you had just seen a supernatural being! In seeing the vision, listening to the angel and later writing it all down, Daniel certainly is serving God. Afterward he gets up and goes about "the king's business," the work assigned to him by the king. (8:27). Daniel moves seamlessly from the supernatural vision to the workplace, because in doing the work of the earthly king, he is still serving God. Is it possible that the slave Daniel might have crossed Paul's mind as he wrote, centuries later, instructing Christian slaves in Colossae to obey their earthly masters, because "it is the Lord Christ you are serving" (Co. 3:24)? Paul too, well-read in Hebrew, knew all about *avad*.

So to Daniel, the Jew, having the same word speak of both work and worship presented no problem. In each and in both, he served God. But that still does not answer the second question:

Why Do We Struggle Seeing Work as Worship? Several factors make it difficult for Christians today to grasp how we might offer our work to God as worship.

The Sacred-Secular Blindfold. Chapter One of this book touches on how we've come to see the world as divided into sacred and secular compartments. This way of thinking distorts the way we view work.

Sacred brings to mind such terms as *pure, holy* and *consecrated*. The Merriam-Webster online dictionary even includes the word worship in its definition of *sacred*: *"dedicated or set apart for the service or worship of a deity."* All these words describe the kinds of things we know please God. So if you engage in *sacred* work, it's easy to think of what you do as worthy of offering as part of your worship.

On the other hand, *secular* gets associated with a completely different set of words. Like *worldly*. Or *profane* (the root word of *profanity*). Or *materialistic*. One atheistic group calls its website the Secular Web. So if you think of your work as *secular*, you won't see much potential for offering it as worship.

The New Testament, however, never labels some work as sacred and other work as secular. It does say that God has—ahead of time—prepared Christians to do *good* works (Eph. 2:10). Paul, in writing to slaves about their work, does not call it *secular*. Instead he encourages them to do their work wholeheartedly, because the Lord will reward them for the *good* they do (Eph. 6:7). So through our widespread use of the unbiblical categories of sacred work versus secular work, we make it extremely difficult for janitors, retail clerks or software developers to see their work as worship.

The Bad Example Barrier. The motives behind the work we typically see and read about only add to our difficulty. News media spotlight people in the business world who lie and cheat and cook the books to make themselves rich. Many ordinary people who never make the headlines hate their jobs, but stay with them anyway. Why? To buy toys to play with on weekends. To build palatial houses. To fund "cushy" retirements. Or to climb corporate ladders. So much of the work we see done in the world today is offered on the altar of greed or ambition. The sheer volume of this idolatrous work can make it difficult to see that, as a citizen of God's kingdom, a Christian may offer his or her work as acceptable worship to him.

The Distracted Mind Confusion. One other misunderstanding that prevents us from seeing work this way is the idea that in worship I must focus my thoughts exclusively on God. Suppose my work requires me to concentrate on writing a sales report, repairing a refrigerator or operating a backhoe. Do those divert my attention away from God and so cancel any worship? I have known Christians who fill their work spaces with Christian posters, books, plaques, artwork and recordings of Christian music—all in an attempt to keep themselves focused on things above while doing what their job requires here below. Am I saying it's wrong to keep a Bible on your desk or display Bible verses on a screensaver? No. My point is that as a Christian you don't have to do a work-station-to-chapel makeover to offer your work as worship.

Your worship as a Christian does not originate in your mind or emotions. Phil. 3:3 reveals that we "worship by the Spirit of God" (NIV) or "we worship God by means of his Spirit" (TEV). We cannot come up with our own salvation. God saves us by means of Jesus' death and resurrection. Neither can we come up with our own worship. God produces our worship by means of his Spirit who lives in us. God's Spirit continues to live in you even when you go off to work in a completely irreligious environment. And though your job requires you to give your full mental attention to adjusting an insurance claim, reviewing a job application or navigating a bus through city traffic, you can still—by means of God's Spirit active in you—be offering your work as worship. Doing so, then, becomes an act of faith.

Kamalini Kumar (RN, MA), an education instructor for the Samaritan Health System in Clinton, Iowa, discovered the unity of work and worship in her nursing role:

"Worship and work should never become two different things. We worship when we work and we work when we worship, especially when our work is derived from God. It tells us in Genesis that in the beginning God went to work, and what he created was for his purpose and glory. In the second scene we see that man and woman were placed in the garden as workers responsible to God for both fellowship and work.

"Nursing is my profession, my daily work. But it is also an

important way I worship God. For me, work and worship have become like two blades of a scissors; one is useless without the other. I now see that work is a ministry performed before God.

"As I asked God to help me get to know him better, I realized that unless I lived every area of my life in direct obedience to him, my knowledge of him was going to be incomplete and mediocre. I prayed that I would be consumed by God and not by work. I also prayed that I would be as Christ to everyone I meet during the course of the day, and that I would see Christ in them (Mt. 25:45). I fervently asked that my identity would come from being in Christ and not from being a teacher, a nurse or a friend, spouse, mother or any other role.

"After that prayer, I discovered that my attitude of worship grew as I committed each person and the circumstances of each day to God. The quality of my work did not change nor did my dedication to it, but I changed in the way I reacted to the daily grind, the crises, the interruptions and the disappointments. The way I prayed for and treated people changed. I realized I had never prayed for some people I saw every day of my life. That quickly changed. God did something in me I never thought possible after so many years of doing the same thing. I looked forward to each day as a new adventure with him. He gave me many opportunities to minister, to share my faith, to give a reason for the hope that was within me, to lift burdens and to encourage others. I was made wiser, richer and stronger for it." (*Permission* obtained from the Journal of Christian Nursing, vol. 16, number 2, spring 1999, *www.journalofchristiannursing.com*)

Kamalini has discovered what Brother Lawrence knew in the 17th century: "The time of business does not with me differ from the time of prayer, and in the noise and clatter of my kitchen, while several persons are at the same time calling for different things, I possess God in as great tranquility as if I were upon my knees at the blessed sacrament."

Real Worship: Antidote to Worshiping Work.

Knowing truth puts us at risk. Distort it even slightly and the twisted version can mislead, enslave and even ruin. So we need to take care not to use the truth of *work as worship* as an excuse to *worship our work*. Like anything else on earth, work can turn too quickly into an idol. More accurately, the work itself doesn't do the turning. Rather we can turn it into a substitute god. In western culture we tag those who practice this idolatry with other labels— such as *workaholic* or *overachiever*. Workaholics find it hard to cut loose from work. They think about it constantly—even in non-work settings.

Ancient people made idols out of wood, stone or metal. Today, just as our boat-building is more sophisticated, so is our idol-making. I found this testimony on a website: "When I started my professional career, I 'worshiped' my work which I created with my hands and mind. It defined me. I did not attend church for five years. I was not the same person I had been earlier in life. I was not happy; I had lost my purpose." This is classic idolatry. As Is. 2:8 puts it, "Their land is full of idols; they bow down to the work of their hands."

Daniel never shirked his work. Even his enemies couldn't call him a slacker. But while he offered his work as worship, the evidence shows that he did not worship his work. Chapter 6 makes it clear that Daniel made a regular habit of praying three times a day in his upstairs room. Verse 10 says he "went" there, implying that he pushed aside whatever may have been pending in his in-basket and spent time with God. Did he invariably follow this pattern no matter what administrative crisis may have just erupted? Scripture doesn't say. But we do know that he routinely broke away from serving God through his work so that he could serve God by focusing on him without distractions.

I suspect that because Daniel spent time in genuine worship while off duty, he found strength to resist worshiping his work. In real worship, you're presenting yourself to the living, seeing God who lovingly corrects his children. Regularly placing yourself under his gaze when off the job will make you able to offer your work as worship without making it the object of your worship.

I think, too, that if all believers were to see both our work and our worship as *avad*, as serving God, it would end the worship wars. Is it possible that we've been expecting too much out of worship on Sunday? If worship becomes our way of life—even in our work life—maybe we'll lose our desperation to make sure the church music goes exactly to our liking on the weekend.

PUTTING IT TO WORK

- How do you think Christians these days typically define "worship"?
- What difficulties, if any, do you have in thinking of offering God your daily work as worship?
- Describe the effects you may have seen of what this chapter identifies as the Sacred-Secular Blindfold, the Bad Example Barrier or the Distracted Mind Confusion.
- In what ways is your employer—even if not a Christian—serving God in his or her work?
- How can you keep from worshiping your work?

CHAPTER ELEVEN

DISCIPLINE: STAYING SPIRITUALLY FIT

". . . you have to practice spiritual disciplines to have an authentic Christian life in a very secular workplace"
  Peggy Wehmeyer, World Vision

"Full participation in the life of God's Kingdom and in the vivid companionship of Christ comes to us only through appropriate exercise in the disciplines for life in the spirit. Those disciplines alone can become for average Christians 'the conditions upon which the spiritual life is made indubitably real'. . . . There will be a life-giving revolution in our personal lives and in our world."
  Dallas Willard, *The Spirit of the Disciplines*

Framing the Issue: Maintaining a ministry in the workplace requires a spiritually fit Christian, just as running a marathon requires a physically fit athlete. Fitness, whether physical or spiritual, does not come without effort. It takes disciplined training. A close look at how Daniel finished well after many decades in the Babylonian workplace reveals that he practiced spiritual disciplines.

When I began working for the State of Washington, some of my co-workers guessed I'd last only a few weeks. To put it bluntly, they figured my Christian faith was too fragile to survive in the dog-eat-dog political atmosphere of the state capital. They may well have seen me as a hothouse flower transplanted into bug-infested soil scorched by the sun and blasted by the wind. They had good reason to wonder if I'd make it. I had led a sheltered life. As a child in a strong Christian home, I had been surrounded by pray-ing parents, Scripture and high moral standards. Our social circle mostly included friends from our Bible-believing church. After high school, I attended a Christian college, then took a writing job with a publisher of Sunday School materials.

Between youth and adulthood, I struggled with how to invest my life. Part of me, shaped by my Christian subculture, insisted I go into "full-time Christian service." That meant working as a mis-sionary, a pastor or in a Christian organization. The voice urging me to go that way sounded insistent and authoritative. But another voice—quieter and deep inside—called in a different direction. If the Christian faith can't thrive and bear fruit in real-world work, the voice urged, what does it have to say to the vast majority of believers who spend their best hours in such jobs? The struggle went on for some time. Finally, following that inner voice, I applied for and got the state job in Olympia, the Washington State capi-tal. Were my co-workers right? Would the real-world workplace win the day and wash me out?

At some point you too may have asked: How can any Christian maintain a strong faith and an effective witness in one of the world's workplaces? Fifty years ago, our American culture—while not Christian—was at least "Christianized." Even in ordinary workplaces arrangements seemed Christian-friendly. Most busi-nesses closed on Sundays. Schools deferred to church calendars by not scheduling events on Wednesday evenings. But such soci-etal supports have disappeared. Just recently a school ordered a teacher to remove a Bible and all other religious items from his desk. Those in the workplace today deal with a situation similar to what Daniel faced. We have shifted from a culture that defended believers to one that in many ways defies them. Daniel moved from the Holy Land, with its supports for worshiping the true God, to Babylon with its deck stacked for the worship of idols. How did Daniel maintain his faith and witness in that non-supportive work environment? And what can we learn from his example?

Some major changes occur between Daniel 1 and Daniel 6. In chapter 1, the king was Nebuchadnezzar. Now Darius is king. Back then, the Babylonians ruled the world. Now, after overthrowing the Babylonians in 550 B.C., the Persian Empire rules. Back then, Daniel was a young man. Now, more than 60 years later, Daniel is an old guy—perhaps nearing 80. All those years Daniel has worked in various government jobs. So his faith in the true God has stood through time and many tough tests. Here in Daniel 6 we can begin to see his secret of maintaining strong faith and witness in an ungodly work environment.

Daniel Prayed Regularly.

In Chapter Six, we covered the story of Daniel's treacherous co-workers. They conned the king into making it illegal for the next 30 days to pray to anyone except the king himself. News of the new law reached Daniel. Yet three times a day, he went upstairs to his room, knelt in front of open windows facing Jerusalem and prayed to the true God. Verse 11 says he did this "just as he had done before." In other words, the new law didn't change a thing in Daniel's prayer habits. He had made prayer a regular part of his life, just as regular as three meals a day have become for many of us. Even though his job put him in one of the most responsible government positions, he still made time every day—three times a day—for prayer. Here's our first clue as to how Daniel could remain faithful and fruitful in his "secular" job. He found his strength not in outward circumstances but in his inner connection with God.

My granddad owned a peach orchard. When the fruit got heavy, he supported the branches with wooden sticks. These props kept the loaded branches from breaking. When Daniel was ripped from his homeland and relocated in Babylon, all the outward props for his faith disappeared. The Temple, center of Jewish worship—gone. The priesthood and the animal sacrifices—gone. The regular feasts, which drew together Jews from all across the Holy Land—gone. On the job in Babylon, Daniel could not depend on those outward props. Instead, he found strength for his "branch" by cultivating his inward relationship with God through the spiritual discipline of prayer.

In his devotional book, *How to be a Transformed Person*, E. Stanley Jones comments, "A diver who would be too busy to think about getting his pipe line for air in working order before he descends to the depths, would be no more foolish than the man who descends into the stifling atmosphere of today's life without getting his breathing apparatus of prayer connected with the pure air of the Kingdom of God above. If we grow anemic and pale, it is because we have done ourselves this harm—the harm of self-inflicted asphyxiation."

Where did those envious Babylonian officials find their strength? Certainly there was no power in their lifeless false gods. So they scratched and clawed for position and power, even to the point of tricking their king into signing a law he later regretted. They concentrated on getting power in the temporary, earthly kingdom. But, as the defeat of the Babylonian empire had just proved, earthly kingdoms are here today and gone tomorrow. By contrast, Daniel made it his first priority to tap into the power of the kingdom that will last forever. Through regular prayer, Daniel anchored his hope and faith in the permanent kingdom. This is the kingdom the sovereign God will establish over the entire visible world. This is the same kingdom Jesus would later announce we are to seek first and enter even now. Daniel found his source of strength in the King of that unseen kingdom for more than 60 years. That's staying power! And once again, through his now-aging man, God demonstrated his sovereignty. This time by locking the jaws of the hungry lions.

Daniel Studied Scripture.

Chapter 9 gives us a glimpse of another spiritual discipline Daniel maintained even across his long career of working for a pagan government. In 9:2, we read that Daniel "understood from the Scriptures, according to the word of the LORD given to Jeremiah the prophet, that the desolation of Jerusalem would last seventy years." If Daniel had had our chapter-and-verse divisions, he might have pointed us to Jer. 29:10, where that prophet wrote: "This is what the LORD says: When seventy years are completed for Babylon, I will come to you and fulfill my gracious promise to bring you back to this place." And in v. 14, "I will . . . bring you back from captivity."

When Daniel read this Scripture this time, it moved him to prayer. Why? Remember, Daniel is now an old man. It's been 60-plus years since Nebuchadnezzar took him and his friends into captivity. So, as he reads the biblical prophecy, Daniel apparently realizes that the promised 70 years in captivity are nearly over. The point here is that Daniel studied and believed Scripture. This was another spiritual discipline that made him able to grow spiritually even as he worked in a pagan environment. He could patiently carry out his duties as a government worker, because his study of Scripture gave him the big picture. He knew who was going to win in the end. Not Nebuchadnezzar. Not Darius. Not Babylon. Not Persia. But the sovereign God whose permanent kingdom was coming.

Daniel Denied Himself.

So Daniel prayed. He studied Scripture. And in chapters 9 and

10, we find two brief references to a third spiritual discipline: he fasted. After being reminded from Scripture that God would end the captivity after 70 years, Daniel "turned to the Lord God and pleaded with him in prayer and petition, in fasting . . ." (9:3). Two years later, Daniel entered a three-week period of self-denial. "I ate no choice food; no meat or wine touched my lips; and I used no lotions at all until the three weeks were over" (10:3). To concentrate on prayer, Daniel went on a partial food fast. He also gave up skin-conditioning lotions. In other words, to focus more completely on prayer, he denied himself the normal comforts of life. At the end of these three weeks, Daniel had a vision of a visitor from the eternal kingdom. A being that looked like a man but must have been an angel appeared to Daniel and told him of the future in store for Israel.

Daniel's temporary abstinence from choice food, meat and wine suggests that he had not permanently continued the vegetables-only diet mentioned in chapter 1. Perhaps fasting, for him, was something he reserved for special and intense times of prayer. So this working man was not an ascetic who starved himself in normal times. But when the occasion called for it, he was willing to deny himself legitimate pleasures in order to concentrate on the sovereign God who rules the eternal kingdom.

How You Can Thrive at Work.

We've seen how a sheltered, religious youth spent his whole career in a pagan government job and yet grew stronger in his faith and more powerful in his witness. Daniel did it by tapping into the power of the sovereign God, Ruler of the kingdom that will last forever. His spiritual disciplines serve as the lines connecting him with that power. What can you learn from his example?

Make God's eternal kingdom your top priority. Daniel centered his life in God's kingdom centuries before Jesus came and told us to seek it first. Jesus told Nicodemus no one can see or enter the kingdom of God without being spiritually born again. This invisible kingdom is real—just as real as the invisible air you breathe. Someday, God's kingdom will come visibly. Then, his will shall be done on earth, as it is in heaven. But right now, by putting your faith in God's King Jesus, you can enter into the living reality of that kingdom and experience its power on your job.

Keep those positions of workplace power in perspective. Daniel held several positions of power in his government jobs. But by staying in relationship with the King of the eternal kingdom, he saw all earthly positions of power as only temporary. So he didn't engage in office politics to get them or hold them. Simply do your work to make God look good, and leave the results with your real and permanent Boss. You may get promoted. That's okay. Keep making God look good from your new position. But don't fall in love with the status or the power to control others.

Don't depend on church for power to get through your work week. Daniel had known plenty of religious supports in his homeland. But working in Babylon, he had none of them. Far too many Christians think of Sunday church as the place to power up after a grueling week at work. Someone asked a Christian, "What is your favorite day of the week?" The reply: "Sunday—time to go get recharged at church, so I can get through another frantic week." But this is not how Daniel did things. He recharged his batteries not once a week but at least three times every day—not in a special earthly building but in the presence of the King of the eternal kingdom. When you gather with other believers on Sunday, do so to encourage and to be encouraged by them. Fellowship with other believers can refresh our own faith. But don't expect church attendance to provide the power only a living and daily relationship with Christ can provide.

Stay fit for the eternal kingdom by practicing spiritual disciplines. In Daniel we've seen three disciplines: prayer, studying Scripture and self-denial. Follow Daniel's example, but not mechanically. For example, he prayed three times a day. That fit his schedule. It may not fit yours. The discipline in this case is regular prayer, not someone else's schedule. During the years I was working for state government, I often made it a practice to walk and pray during my lunch hour. This removed me from the interruptions of ringing phones and drop-ins and made it possible to focus my attention on conversations with our heavenly Father.

There are many more spiritual disciplines—such as solitude, silence, Scripture memorization, meditation and so on. The spiritual disciplines do not earn you any points with God. You might compare them with physical exercise. Regular workouts will lead you to physical fitness. And when you are physically fit, your body is ready to meet the stresses and demands of life. Through the spiritual disciplines, you can become spiritually fit. Then, like Daniel, you will be ready to meet the tests and pressures of your daily work.

In his book, *The Spirit of the Disciplines*, Dallas Willard writes, "The disciplines for the spiritual life are available, concrete activities designed to render bodily beings such as we ever more sensitive and receptive to the Kingdom of Heaven brought to us in Christ, even while living in a world set against God." The world of work is set against God. But even there you can still stay receptive to God and his kingdom as you practice spiritual disciplines.

Include Your Work Life in your Prayer Life. The Sunday-Monday gap, the false division between the "sacred" world of church and the "secular" world of work, can cramp the territory covered by our prayers. As a result, our prayers may extend to the people, programs and projects connected with the churches we attend, but not to co-workers and job-related issues. Scripture tells us that Daniel thanked God and asked him for help (6:10-11). We don't know the range of petitions he normally included in his three-times-a-day prayer sessions. We do know that on at least one occasion he asked God to intervene in a job-related crisis (2:23). Following his example, part of your discipline of prayer could embrace your work and workplace. For instance, your prayer agenda might include such thanksgivings and requests as these:

- Thanks: That I have a job through which God is supplying me and my family along with enough to share with others.
- Thanks: For the opportunity to use my gifts and skills in work that contributes to God's purposes for maintaining life on planet earth.
- Petition: That my supervisor (or my employer) may be given the wisdom, strength and moral courage required to make the kind of decisions that will result in sound leadership. (Paul urges prayer for "all those in authority" [I Tim. 2:2]. Although the context is government, the word translated "authority" means those in leadership positions.)
- Petition: That I will not be led into temptation as a result of my work or the influence of my co-workers, but that God will continually deliver me from the traps of the evil one. (Matt. 6:13)
- Petition: That God will guide my path into meaningful contact and dialogue with other believers and that he will use me to build them up as members of the body of Christ. (Gal. 6:10)
- Petition: That I will be sensitive to the broken places in the lives of unbelievers (both co-workers and customers) whose lives intersect with mine today—and that I may deal with them gently and with respect. (I Pet. 3:15)
- Petition: That God's Spirit will convict my unbelieving co-workers (fill in their names) of sin, righteousness and judgment, and will grant them the gift of repentance and faith in Christ. (Jn. 16:8-11; II Tim. 2:25; Acts 20:21)
- Petition: That I will be given clear ethical and moral discernment as my work requires me to make decisions that will affect the lives of others. (Eph. 5:15; Col. 4:5)

Contemporary Examples from the Work World.

For more than a half-century I've received Christian instruction from sermons, books, classes and so on. Looking back, I recall that most examples of practicing spiritual disciplines came from the lives of clergy or missionaries. John Hyde, now known as "Praying Hyde," served as a missionary to India. George Mueller, pastor and evangelist, is recognized as making his needs known only to God through prayer. E. M. Bounds, a pastor, prayed every day from 4:00 to 7:00 a.m. Cotton Mather, says one source, "spent hours on his knees." These and many other stories of Christian discipline inspire and encourage. But those who work as clergy or missionaries do not face the same schedule demands as Christians who work in shops, offices, classrooms, factories and fields. But even though we seldom hear about them in sermons and Christian literature, examples from the working world do exist. Sometimes, under the pressures of today's workplaces, the disciplines emerge in new forms.

Brad is Vice President of Assets Protection for a fortune 500 company —responsible for domestic and global security. His challenges and pressures resemble those of many in the corporate workplace: time constraints, travel, personnel issues, etc. He says, "The reality is I could work 12 hours a day, seven days a week, and not close the gap.

"My practice of spiritual disciplines has evolved through the years. Early on my wife and I had read Richard Foster's book, *Celebration of Discipline*, and were involved with discipleship training (church and Navigators). So we practiced several disciplines. As work became more demanding I had to adjust my practices and expectations. I still try to have a few minutes of Scripture reading and prayer in the morning, but this tends to be brief—more like sharing a cup of coffee than a Bible study.

"I have found listening to Christian music—David Crowder, Newsboys, etc.—on the way to work or even early in the office before meetings to be a way to center my thoughts and worship. This has been a change. In the past music on the radio was more to entertain or distract.

"Another practice I have developed is to look for ways each day to recognize people for something they have done or accomplished. Often through email, sometimes in person, it allows me to act or demonstrate concern for others—a way to bring kindness into the workplace. I have found these actions encouraging to others and perhaps a form of worship. It also gives me perspective, a perspective that can be lost in the busy-ness of corporate life.

"We have been blessed to own a cabin in northern Wisconsin. It is there that I can best regain perspective on life and God. To see the millions of stars in a night sky—stars that have been seen by people for thousands of years, stars that have witnessed man's history, stars that exist even though I cannot see them while in my office, on a jet, or in a meeting—it is then I know the greatness of God, His majesty and His power. It is a time of worship for me, a time to reflect, a time of faith.

"In summary my disciplines have become diversified or eclectic—not in forms I originally learned or practiced—but forms that help me refocus on God and keep the world around me in perspective."

As a Christian, Peggy Wehmeyer saw the need for accurate reporting of faith-based stories while working in the public relations department of Dallas Theological Seminary. Her contacts in that role led to ten years as a reporter for WFAA-TV in Dallas. In 1994, the late Peter Jennings supported ABC News in hiring Peggy as the first religion correspondent to work full-time with a national news network. In a recent interview, Peggy was asked, "What spiritual disciplines got you through network television reporting?" Her answer:

"These are imperative; you can't stress these things enough. First, to stay in the struggle—and it is a struggle—have regular time apart with God. That was a big struggle, but I could always tell a difference in my life when I did and when I didn't. To stay centered with God, you have to have a regular consistent time of prayer and meditation—prayer and exposure to Scripture.

"The second thing—for me, almost as important—was intimate fellowship and accountability with a small group. Like regular time with God, you need regular time with a small group of people who will pray with you, hold you accountable, and accept you unconditionally—the body of Christ.

"Those were the two main things that kept me on track spiritually . . . kept me anchored."

Similar disciplines kept me receptive in my state job. Yes—in contrast to the predictions of some co-workers—I did last for more than a few weeks. In fact, I continued as a state employee for the next 11 years. And you too, wherever you work, can not only survive but thrive spiritually as you take heart from Daniel's example of sustaining your working life with spiritual disciplines. But those disciplines can die in the suffocating atmosphere of legalism unless you're consistently drawing on the renewing power of the Holy Spirit—the focus of Chapter Eleven.

PUTTING IT TO WORK

- In his book, *The Spirit of the Disciplines*, Dallas Willard says, "The disciplines are activities of mind and body purposefully undertaken to bring our personality and total being into effective cooperation with the divine order." Do you agree or disagree with this definition of spiritual disciplines? Tell why.
- In your experience as a believer, what spiritual disciplines have proved most helpful in sustaining your faith and walk in the workplace?
- Identify any disciplines you've never practiced that you believe could contribute to your spiritual fitness for a workplace ministry.

- To what degree might you have been depending on a weekly church service to "recharge your batteries" for the week to come?
- What obstacles have you encountered in attempting to practice spiritual disciplines? What have you done (are you doing) to overcome these barriers?

CHAPTER TWELVE

POWER: Being Filled with the Holy Spirit

"The Spirit of God calls, endows, and empowers Christians to work in their various vocations. . . . Christians should understand their mundane work as 'work in the Spirit' . . . ."
    Miroslav Volf, Work in the Spirit

"While Jesus is at the throne as head of the church, the power of the Holy Spirit is the heart of the church at work."
    A. B. Simpson, The Spirit-Filled Church in Action

Framing the Issue: Christian leaders often speak about the need for God's people to be empowered. Carrying on a workplace ministry takes far more power than any of us can generate on our own. Yet it's all too easy to begin thinking the empowerment comes from top-notch training or well planned programs. Daniel's power came from being filled with the Holy Spirit—a gift now available to all who come to God through Christ.

The church was nearly 20 years old, and the man who led the team that planted it had served as its pastor since its beginning. At an annual meeting, the pastor announced plans to begin asking elders and other qualified believers to share in bringing the Sunday messages. But one church member stood up and took exception. "How can they preach?" he asked. "They've never attended seminary." The pastor—who had a fairly close relationship with the man—smiled and said, "Neither have I."

Although this true story comes not from the workplace but from an organized church, it illustrates a widely held idea that greatly affects Christians in so-called "secular" jobs. When believers put this attitude into words, it often comes out sounding much like an apology. For example, a Christian blogger starts out his comments like this: "I have not attended seminary (which is probably obvious to some of you). I have not taken any class on either exegesis or hermeneutics. I don't read Greek, Hebrew, Aramaic or Latin." Another example: "I am not a trained theologian. I have not attended seminary. I have not had classes on 'exegesis' (look that up). I have no formal training on the scholarly examination of the Bible." Such statements focus on the *have nots*.

Attitudes work their way into applications. Too often this kind of thinking trickles into life along these lines: "I'm lacking seminary (Greek, exegesis, homiletics, or what have you). Therefore, I am not qualified for real spiritual ministry. How egotistical if I thought I could speak with any credibility on matters involving God, the Bible or someone else's soul. So I'll leave the heavy lifting of ministry to those who have the degrees and credentials to back them up."

To some, then, *workplace ministry*—even if it were possible—seems wrong. For non-seminarians to engage in *ministry* in the *workplace* seems like practicing surgery without benefit of medical school. But here again, Daniel's experience in the workplace can shed some corrective light.

What the Babylonians Saw in Daniel.

After Nebuchadnezzar's frightening dream about the massive tree, he called in Babylon's brain trust—the magicians, enchanters, astrologers and diviners—for an interpretation. But the dream stumped them. So the king called in Daniel, his best dream-unraveler. Just before detailing the dream for Daniel, Nebuchadnezzar told him, "I know that the spirit of the holy gods is in you, and no mystery is too difficult for you" (4:9). In 4:18, just after telling Daniel his dream, the king repeats the same explanation of Daniel's ability to untangle the meaning of dreams: ". . . the spirit of the holy gods is in you."

Decades later, another king encounters another puzzle (Daniel 5). The new monarch, Belshazzar, doesn't know of Daniel or his interpretive abilities. So when fingers scratch out a mysterious message in the wall plaster, and when his experts can't decipher it, Belshazzar has no clue what to do. Just in time, the queen recalls that Daniel, now an old man, had demonstrated an ability to solve such puzzles. Daniel, said the queen, "has the spirit of the holy gods in him" (5:11). When attendants brought Daniel, the king explains, "I have heard that the spirit of the gods is in you" (5:14).

We should not read our own meaning into what these pagan idol-worshipers said. In speaking of "the spirit of the holy gods," they reflected their frame of reference, Babylonian polytheism. They were not referring to the third person of the Holy Trinity. Yet what they said is significant, because they used the only terms they knew in trying to describe what they saw in Daniel. Daniel's ability to grasp unseen meanings could only come, they thought, from the "holy gods," from powers completely set apart from and beyond the human reach. And, at least to that extent, they were right.

What they did *not* say is also significant. Daniel had been trained in "the language and the literature of the Babylonians." In *The NIV Application Commentary*, Tremper Longman III writes that, "Daniel clearly would have been trained in the arts of divination

. . . .Divination was a learned practice in that portended events were associated with certain signs (like symptoms of an illness), whether the shape of a liver, unusual births, the flight pattern of birds, the stars or dreams. Diviners used reference books to tease out the significance of the sign. . . .But the reference books only helped diviners interpret dreams that the subject narrated to them. They did not have the tools to discover the contents of a dream if the subject chose, for whatever reason, to withhold that information." Daniel had graduated summa cum laude from the Babylonian educational system. But neither Nebuchadnezzar nor (years later) the queen claimed that Daniel's powers came from the education they had given him. They recognized that his gift-edness came not from books or human teachers. It had to come from a supernatural outside source.

Now, 2,600 years after Daniel, we Christians often explain successful ministry in terms of schools attended, degrees attained, books read and titles conferred. Many assume that if you want to "enter the ministry" (working as a religious professional), you had best enroll in a seminary—or at least a Bible college. Although Daniel was not a religious professional, who can deny that he carried on a fruitful ministry via his workplace in Babylon? Yet as a teenager, he had not completed advanced theological training before his forced move to a strange land. He did not arrive in Babylon as Doctor Daniel. Like the Babylonians, we cannot explain Daniel's giftedness in terms of his academic training.

Please understand I am not arguing against attending seminary or Bible college. For some Christians, such training provides exactly the preparation they need for what God has called them to do. But academic training from those sources does not fit great numbers of those for whom the workplace is the ministry setting. Should they receive instruction in theology and spiritual care? Yes. But why not make such training available to them locally in formats and at a cost accessible to them?

What Empowered Daniel for Workplace Ministry?

Had Daniel remained in his homeland, we can speculate that he might have taken formal training in theology. But such guided study was not an option for him in Babylon. From what source, then, did Daniel receive his power for workplace ministry?

In a way far greater than the Babylonians understood, Daniel indeed got his power from an outside, supernatural Source— from the Holy Spirit of the true God. It's true, of course, that in Daniel's day the mighty outpouring of the Holy Spirit, foretold in Jl. 2:28-29, was still centuries in the future, in the A.D. years. But the Spirit of God worked in B.C. times too. For example, the Old Testament repeatedly speaks of the Spirit of the Lord coming upon individuals. Because the Spirit of the Lord came upon Caleb's nephew, Othniel, he was able to serve as Israel's judge and lead the nation to victory in war. That same anointing by the Spirit of God explains the triumphs of Gideon, Jephthah, Samson, Saul, David and many more.

The Bible never says that the "Spirit of the Lord came upon" Daniel in those exact words. But Daniel authored Scripture, so we know that he was "carried along by the Holy Spirit" (II Pet. 1:21). Did the Spirit of God visit Daniel only on those "spiritual" occasions when he received prophetic visions and dreams? Or was Daniel filled with God's Spirit even while creating policies, training supervisors and overseeing building projects for the government? Is God interested enough in regular work to fill those doing it with his Spirit? Consider Bezalel, a master craftsman God used in building the Tabernacle, who lived some 800 years before Daniel. God says of Bezalel, "I have filled him with the Spirit of God, with skill, ability and knowledge in all kinds of crafts" (Ex. 31:3). To my mind, only one explanation for Daniel's exceptional work makes sense: he lived and did his everyday work under the control and in the power of the Holy Spirit. Daniel, the Spirit-filled bureaucrat working in a secular government, blazed a trail you can follow today right where you work.

To some of us, Spirit-filling and everyday working seem to occupy separate universes. We might even echo the question raised by theologian Miroslav Volf: "But what does the Spirit of God have to do with the mundane work of human beings?" (*Work in the Spirit*). In response to that question, Volf answers that a biblically accurate understanding of work requires a Spirit-oriented theology of work. "Because the whole creation is the Spirit's sphere of operation," he says, "the Spirit is not only the Spirit of religious experience but also the Spirit of worldly engagement." He continues, "the Spirit of God calls, endows, and empowers Christians to work in their various vocations. . . . All human work, however complicated or simple, is made possible by the operation of the Spirit of God in the working person."

A Gift Beyond What Daniel Knew.

While Daniel knew and worked in the power of God's Spirit, we believers today have the promise of even more. Now that Jesus has died, risen and returned to his Father in heaven, he has poured out the Holy Spirit just as Joel prophesied. The very day of that outpouring, Peter counseled the crowd to repent and be baptized in Jesus' name. Two blessings would follow—forgiveness of sins and the "gift of the Holy Spirit." This gift was for them, their children and everyone everywhere. And as Jesus had promised, the Holy Spirit would teach, guide into truth and empower his followers. The promise still stands and the power of the Holy Spirit still works.

But many things that still work as well as ever seem to have gone out of fashion. Sharp handsaws. Crank-handle ice cream churns. Wise parenting. A parent wrote to a parenting expert complaining about a son who forgets everything he is told to do. The expert advice? An old-fashioned remedy known as *discipline*. Post a list of privileges. Take one away each time the boy forgets a chore. If pursued consistently, this practice will remarkably improve his memory. In many Christian circles teaching on being filled with the Holy Spirit seems to have disappeared. Yes, according to the New Testament it's right at the heart of living out and serving in the Christian life. But other emphases have crowded this vital truth to the sidelines.

As a result, many believers who hold to the promise of forgiven sin have not learned to live by the promise of the outpoured Holy Spirit. That was true of me in my first so-called "secular" job. Although I had been a Christian for 20 years, I had never been challenged to pray for and expect the filling of the Holy Spirit. But God used on-the-job pressures, timed with some excellent teaching, to lead me to begin claiming the promise. How many are trying to live for Christ in their regular jobs—but doing so in their own strength? How many think their lack of seminary or Bible-college training disqualifies them for ministry in the workplace? How many believers in the workplaces of this world need to be filled with the Holy Spirit?

The Gift Belongs to All Believers. God gives the gift of his outpoured Spirit not only to pastors but also to plumbers, not only to missionaries but also to mechanics, not only to Christian counselors but also to Christian computer programmers. When Paul instructed the believers in Ephesus to "be filled with the Spirit," he followed up almost immediately by addressing wives and husbands, children, fathers, and slaves and employers (Eph. 5:18-6:9). So God intends that all his people constantly live by the power of the Holy Spirit in their everyday roles—including their work lives.

God used several books by Andrew Murray in the process of my spiritual formation. For me, *The Spirit of Christ* turned out to be one of the most life-shaping of his books. In that book, Murray clarifies this matter of Spirit-filling. Murray—writing in South Africa, and in English now over 100 years old—can sometimes be difficult to follow for 21st century readers. So I'll attempt to paraphrase a section from *The Spirit of Christ* that particularly helped me to understand Eph. 5:18, "Be filled with the Spirit . . . ."

To be filled with the Spirit is a privilege all believers may claim. Only this makes us able to live the life God redeemed us for—remaining in Christ, obeying his commands and bearing much fruit. Yet few see this be-filled command as one for every Christian to keep.

Why? Probably because we have misunderstood the words. We associate them with the day of Pentecost and other times when those who were filled with the Spirit displayed spectacular enthusiasm, joy and power. So we think being filled must be exciting and strenuous—hardly fitting the circumstances of everyday life. The filling of the Spirit, so closely linked with the spectacular signs, led many to think the blessing was for just a few. It seemed out of reach for them. But the command, the promise and the power are for every believer.

The Gift Arrives in Different Ways. As I tried to understand how to recognize the working of God in gifting us with his Spirit, the variety of the teaching I encountered confused me. Some spoke of the "filling of the Spirit" and the "baptism of the Spirit" and the "anointing by the Spirit" interchangeably. Others insisted on drawing a distinction among those terms. Some held that salvation and Spirit-filling were two distinct experiences. Others insisted both happened at conversion. Some said the experience always came with stunning supernatural signs, while others said such manifestations were not necessary. Once again, Andrew Murray's writings came to my rescue. In The Spirit of Christ, he illustrates how the filling of the Spirit sometimes comes quietly and sometimes more dramatically. My paraphrase of that section follows:

In South Africa we often suffer from drought. Farmers catch and store water two ways. Some farms have springs—but the flow is too weak for irrigation. In these cases, farmers make reservoirs to collect the spring water as it flows gently and quietly day and night. On farms without springs the farmers also build reservoirs, but they do so to collect rainwater. A downpour of rain can fill the reservoir in just a few hours—sometimes with a rushing, danger-ous gushing stream. The quiet spring-fed reservoir provides more reliable irrigation, because even though the supply may be feeble it is permanent. However, on farms where rainfall may or may not come, the reservoir might sit empty for months or years.

The fullness of the Spirit can come in two similar ways. On the day of Pentecost and in times of new beginnings, the outpouring of the Spirit may come suddenly, powerfully and visibly. In the excite-ment and joy of freshly found salvation, the power of the Spirit is obviously present. But such cases bring unique risks. People often depend too much on fellowship with others. Or the experience proves to be superficial, not reaching the core of the will and inner life.

Other Christians never have such a dramatic experience. Yet they show the fullness of the Spirit in their deep and intense de-votion to Jesus. They walk in the light, are conscious of Christ's presence and live blameless lives of trust and obedience and love for others.

Which of these is the right way of being filled with the Spirit? The analogy of spring-fed and rain-fed reservoirs makes the an-swer easy. Some Christians must have the dramatic fillings: the rushing wind, downpours, and fire are their symbols. Others, with the quiet, internal fountain, see this as the true work of God's Spirit. Still others can recognize God in both kinds of filling and stay ready to let him bless them either way.

The Gift Empowers in Various Ways. We receive the gift of the Holy Spirit's fullness by faith. But yet another misunder-standing can block faith from claiming this gift for the workplace. Believers long-immersed in the programs and traditions of the typical church may have picked up the signal that the Holy Spirit empowers only "sacred" or "church-related" work. They may think that being filled with the Spirit has nothing to do with installing a furnace, preparing an invoice or managing an office staff.

A passage from Andrew Murray's *Abide in Christ* seems especially helpful in clearing up this misunderstanding. Once again, what follows is my paraphrase:

The baptism of power came to qualify believers for the work to which they had given themselves, whether witnessing by their lives or by their words.

With some, the main witness is that of a holy life—a life reflecting both heaven and the Christ who came from it. In these believers, the power comes to set up the Kingdom of God within them. It gives victory over sin and self. It fits them by living experience to show forth the power of Jesus on his throne to make people able to live as saints in the world.

Others devote themselves entirely to speaking in the name of Jesus. But all needed and received the gift of power . . . whether for a holy life or effective service.

What is Murray saying? Not all Spirit-empowered ministries will look like what we've come to expect in a worship service or a church outreach program. While those ministries focus on *speaking* the message, other ministries—such as those in workplaces—will mostly require *living it out*. Time-wise, the ministries of Jeremiah and Daniel overlapped. Suppose you could thumb through a schedule book for each man. Jeremiah's would probably contain page after page of speaking engagements. It would also include preparing object-lessons such as hiding a linen belt, breaking a clay jar and buying a field, Daniel's book would likely show staff meetings, hiring interviews, budget-reviews—as well as a few last-minute dream-interpretation and wall-reading sessions. Both men had ministries. But each invested his God-given time in different activities. Jeremiah worked among those who professed faith. Daniel worked among outright unbelievers. Ministry in the *gathered* church will contrast greatly with ministry in the *scattered* church in the workplace. But neither can happen effectively without the power and fullness of the Holy Spirit.

The Gift Worth Asking For.

But just knowing that God gives the Holy Spirit to all his children—including those in the workplaces of the world—is not enough. Understanding that the outward signs of the filling with God's Spirit appear in a variety of ways is not enough. Nor is it enough to believe that God fills with his Spirit to empower believers for greatly contrasting ministries. Grasping all these truths will clear away some of the barriers that prevent you from being filled. But the bottom line is this: *you personally need to be filled with God's Spirit.* But how?

The book of Daniel does not answer the how question directly. But in a work-related situation already described in Chapter Two, we see a pattern that points us in the right direction. The king's execution order included Daniel and his three Jewish friends. Naturally, Daniel saw this as a "harsh decree" (2:15). He asked for a grace period and gathered with his friends in a prayer huddle. What motivated Daniel and his friends to meet for prayer? Their *need.* And what did they do in that huddle? They *pled.* Pled for mercy concerning the unknown dream of the king. And God, presumably by means of the vision-giving Holy Spirit, revealed the mystery that same night.

What's the pattern? *Needing* and *pleading.* Those two words provide a simple yet effective answer to the question, *How can someone in the workplace be filled with the Holy Spirit?*

The will of God, expressed in the biblical command, "Be filled with the Spirit," creates the needing. Those words tell me what God expects me to be full of as I meet the challenges in my work day. But if I'm honest, I have to admit that I'm all too often full of myself instead of God's Spirit. The fruit of his Spirit does not grow in the orchard of my self-life. Some mornings, it's all I can do to drag myself to work, let alone love my co-workers as I love myself. Missed deadlines, broken promises and shoddy work all call for far more patience than my self-life can produce. And when someone else gets assigned to the project I deserved, my reaction (even if known only by my insides) shows a distinct lack of self-control. So there I am—*needing* to be filled with the Spirit from whom those qualities naturally grow.

God, of course, always supplies anything he requires. So the next step is to couple his command with his promise. Jesus embedded just such a promise in the context of some teaching on persistent asking. After noting that even flawed human fathers respond favorably to their children's requests, he said, "If you then, though you are evil, know how to give good gifts to your children, how much more will your Father in heaven give the Holy Spirit to those who ask him" (Lk. 11:13). So Jesus encourages the *pleading*.

Several years ago my family dramatized needing and pleading in a way I've never forgotten. The five of us were driving north on Interstate-5, heading home to Washington State after vacationing in southern California. The summer sun had turned the San Joaquin Valley into an oven, and our small Volkswagen Rabbit—with no air-conditioning—felt like the roasting pan. The chorus of complaints from our dehydrating children had been swelling in volume and intensity for miles. But somewhere between Sacramento and Redding, the demand from the parched throats reached its peak. I realized that unless I acted quickly, I'd have to deal with a mutiny. Their needing prompted their pleading. And, as a father who knew how to give good gifts to his children, I took the very next exit and found them ice water.

The heat generated through your work can bake you hard, or it can create intense thirst for the living water of the Holy Spirit—the *needing*. That thirst, banking on the promise of God, produces the passionate asking—the *pleading*. Authentic ministry in your workplace does not require that you graduate from a seminary, complete requirements for ordination, or train at a Bible college—as valuable as each of these can be. Circumstances or finances may put these completely out of reach. But you and every believer may claim the promises of God to be filled, taught, led and made productive by the Holy Spirit. Does this rule out any need for training and disciplined study? Certainly not. The Holy Spirit will empower such preparation.

On a visit to Israel, my wife and I rode the cable car to the top of Masada—the massive rock mountain that rises roughly 1500 feet above the western shore of the Dead Sea. Aside from the ancient ruins of Herod's hideaways, the 23-acre plateau at the top was nothing but rock and sun-bleached desert sand. As we walked across the bleak landscape, I snapped a picture of something I had not expected to see. Out of the rock rubble was growing a green shrub—thriving life surrounded by deadness. Somehow, the roots of that plant had found their way to an invisible source of water. I still have that picture. It reminds me of Daniel. Planted in the midst of spiritual death, he had tapped into what Ps. 46:4 calls the "river whose streams make glad the city of God, the holy place where the Most High dwells." He had found the "streams of living water" which Jesus would later identify as the Holy Spirit (Jn. 7:38-39).

Only the generous presence of the Holy Spirit explains how Daniel remained true to the sovereign God all across his long career. His vision of the eternal kingdom, his awareness of his own identity and his resistance to corruption all flowed from the Spirit of God within him. His power to do his earth-tending work and to do it in a way that reflected the way God works took more than human willpower. His oneness with fellow believers on the job as well as his love for pagan unbelievers remind us that such love is, as Paul explains, "the fruit of the Spirit." Like Stephen hundreds of years later, Daniel was "full of faith and of the Holy Spirit." His worship was "by the Spirit of God." And the self-control displayed in his spiritual disciplines in Bible study and prayer could have come only from the ongoing presence of the Spirit of God.

From my earliest childhood I can remember singing "Dare to be a Daniel." While the song carries a valuable spur toward taking a courageous stand for God, I wouldn't advise anyone to take the dare at face value. Daniel was Daniel. David was David. Paul was Paul. And you are you. Instead, I dare you to be you, yourself, right there in your workplace. Look to Daniel as a mentor. But let God develop you and your ministry in the way that belongs uniquely to you.

As a Christian, you are a portable "tent" where God's Spirit lives. Every dry and darkened workplace in the Babylon of today's world cries out for the living water and the light that only the presence of the sovereign God can supply. And you, like Daniel, have the high privilege of carrying his life-giving, light-shining presence into the very heart of that thirst-filled darkness. For you to be sent into your workplace in today's Babylon is a privilege—a high and holy calling.

PUTTING IT TO WORK

- What comments have you heard from Christians suggesting that only those with the proper credentials (such as formal theological training or ordination) qualify to carry out real ministry?
- Think back over the teaching you have received as a believer. How much importance has it placed on being filled with the Holy Spirit? Explain why you think this emphasis has been too much, not enough or just right?
- Why do you think Jesus compared the presence of the Holy Spirit in the believer with "steams of living water"? Relate your answer to the needs of the believer in the workplace.
- How does Andrew Murray's farm reservoir analogy speak to you? Which kind of reservoir best represents your experience to date?
- How will you apply what you've read in this chapter? When will you apply it?

LaVergne, TN USA
04 May 2010
181468LV00003B/10/P